Praise for
HAPPY TOGETHER

"*Happy Together* explains why love, like happiness, is an inside job. Dr. Bill Cloke gives great insights into how to create a loving relationship that lasts."

—MARCI SHIMOFF, #1 *New York Times* bestselling
author of *Happy for No Reason*

"Bill Cloke is a genius at showing us how to make the relationship of our dreams more than just a dream. His step-by-step approach for dealing with the most important and sensitive of relationship issues brings us hope that we *can* develop the skills we need to make our relationships thrive. Especially key are his sections throughout on how to understand our personal pain and that of our partner and then use the conflicts that naturally ensue to create what we all long for—a deeply loving and intimate connection. If you are serious about wanting to create and share a truly meaningful love, this book is for you. *Happy Together* is a genuinely beautiful and practical work that should be every couple's companion for a lifetime."

—PATRICIA SPADARO, author of *Honor Yourself:*
The Inner Art of Giving and Receiving

"This book is a must read for those wishing for loving relationships that work! Bill Cloke is a master of practical methods for cultivating intimacy and love. He reveals the deeper causes of problems we face with loved ones and he offers success stories of couples he has treated and solutions we can apply in our own lives."

—DR. JOAN GOLDSMITH, author of *Learning to Lead:*
A Work

D1112971

"A good book needs to have at least five great ideas about its subject. Dr. Bill Cloke's *Happy Together* has at least a hundred."

—RAPHAEL CUSHNIR, author of *The One Thing Holding You Back: Unleashing the Power of Emotional Connection*

"Dr. Bill Cloke provides an accurate portrait of how love is created and nourished. This is a must-have book for a lasting relationship."

—DR. CAROL BRUESS and ANNA KUDAK, authors of *What Happy Couples Do*

happy together

happy together

CREATING A LIFETIME OF CONNECTION, COMMITMENT, AND INTIMACY

Bill Cloke, PhD

Pacific Highlands Press

For information, address:
Pacific Highlands Press
10350 Santa Monica Blvd., Suite 300
Los Angeles, CA 90025
www.pacifichighlandspress.com

For foreign and translation rights, contact Nigel J. Yorwerth
E-mail: nigel@publishingcoaches.com

Library of Congress Control Number: 2010939789

ISBN: 978-0-9829324-1-4

10 9 8 7 6 5 4 3 2 1

Cover design: Nita Ybarra
Interior design: Alan Barnett Design

Distributed by SCB Distributors.

To my wife, Angie, and my daughter, Kristen

Loving someone is knowing the song in their heart
and singing it to them whenever it begins to fade.

—Unknown

CONTENTS

ACKNOWLEDGEMENTS

I thank my mother, Shirley Cloke, for being an indomitable spirit of positive energy and a loving, supportive, and eternally loyal mom. She remains my very dearest friend.

To my beautiful daughter, Kristen, who grew up with me and with her loving honesty and patience encouraged me to become a therapist.

To my brilliant wife, Angie, who inspired me to write this book, put up with me through all the years of writing it, and loved me for all the right reasons. Her vulnerability and loyalty have been the spirit that has given me the strength to finish this project.

To my professors and mentors Drs. Ted Carpenter, Council Taylor, Avendis Panajian, Jack Delchamps, Russell Hunter, Susan Johnson, Daniel Wile, John Gottman, Bill Ofman, and Beverly Frank, and to Vida Van Brunt, John Huston, and Martin Beaudet. To Dr. Esther Benton, whose intelligence, compassion, and love have been a model for what it means to be authentic and caring.

To my accomplished brother, Ken Cloke, and his wife, Joan Goldsmith, for setting the bar that inspired me to do my best work, and for lending their support to this project.

A special thanks to Rick Richman for lending his support and ideas to this book.

I'm eternally grateful to my editor, Anne Barthel, whose professionalism, consummate editorial skills, and inventive mind have given life to this manuscript.

This project could not have come to fruition without the steady hand and expert advice of Nigel J. Yorwerth and Patricia Spadaro, my publishing consultants at PublishingCoaches.com. Their support and professional knowledge have been invaluable.

To my remarkable patients who have over the years taught me so much about perseverance, tolerance, and love. They have given me my most valuable insights, which have enabled me to become a better therapist. The vignettes in this book are composites of people I have worked with and the names and specifics have been changed to protect their privacy.

Thank you all.

the happiness c.u.r.e.

Oh, the comfort—the inexpressible comfort of feeling safe with a person—having neither to weigh thoughts nor measure words, but pouring them all right out, just as they are, chaff and grain together; certain that a faithful hand will take and sift them, keep what is worth keeping, and then with the breath of kindness blow the rest away.

—Dinah Maria Mulock Craik

IT WAS A HOT SUMMER DAY in Santa Monica back in 1983 when Jake and Brenna walked into my office for their weekly therapy session. I was testing my new video recorder and wanted to try it out on them. With their permission, I started it rolling.

They were an attractive couple in their mid-40s who had been married just two years when their conflicts began to escalate. Jake seemed bewildered when they arrived, so I asked him what was bothering him. They had quarreled earlier that day, and he couldn't grasp why Brenna was so upset. She had accused him of raging at her about money, and she told me she did not feel good about the way he had spoken to her. Jake denied raging and insisted that he was only trying to make his point. He was making one excuse after another.

About half an hour into their discussion with me, Brenna blurted out, "Jake, you are just so cheap!" Jake, who had forgotten about the camera, bolted upright, screaming, "How dare you say that when all you do is spend, spend, spend!" He launched into a tirade that left Brenna in tears.

They had been down this road before, always with the same outcome. Brenna melted into the sofa and wept while Jake raged. This was their dance, and it was disastrous for them both. As they were leaving, I handed Jake the videotape to review before our next session.

The next day Jake phoned me, horrified. He sputtered, "Who was that on the tape?" It was shocking to realize that he did not recognize himself as he was in the video. How could this be? I was filled with curiosity about how he could be so blind to himself. It wasn't the first time I had seen such a contradiction in action: although Jake's behavior was extreme, I had observed the same pattern in other patients who couldn't see how they were expressing their personal issues to others.

I began searching for answers to the questions raised by Jake's encounter with his wife and with himself. How can someone experience a powerful emotion like rage and not be aware of it? Why do some relationships withstand rage—or loneliness or infidelity or loss—while others break apart? How can we heal the pain that divides us from the ones we love? Ultimately, what does it take for us to be happy together?

Since that day, in three decades as a psychotherapist and couples counselor, I have searched for answers to these questions in the varied experiences of patients who have come to me for help in making their relationships work, and in nearly 20 years as a husband, I have learned how to make our relationship work, or, quite frankly, I could not have written this book. I have seen firsthand what makes love last. *Happy Together* is the result of these explorations.

Watching the unveiling of the intricate workings of intimacy—of the process by which lasting love is created and sustained—has convinced me that love works on a far grander scale than eyes meeting across a crowded room. Happiness is not something that just happens to us, and love is not something that we just fall into, even though it may seem that way when a relationship begins. No matter how much passion there is at the start, for love and happiness to last a lifetime, they must be actively *made*. Love is a creation; it is fashioned by acts of loving kindness, which can produce something that is at once durable and a thing of beauty. Creating a happy and enduring relationship requires that we understand how our underlying and often baffling personal issues impact our ability to connect with others—and, crucially, with ourselves. It calls on us to make conflict and personal pain into resources for ever deeper intimacy.

Love is an unparalleled life experience. When we accept that it will include times of great difficulty, we can approach them with gentleness and care, and we can learn the skills we need to quickly and smoothly solve problems. Love is what life is all about, and it is life's sweetest reward—the cake and the icing on the cake. It's a flame that can indeed burn for a lifetime, if we tend it well.

Our journey toward enduring love and lasting happiness begins by developing a solid base of safety and security. We set out equipped with honesty, tolerance, and a willingness to reach out to each other when we need to. The path is paved by our intention to solve problems with reasoning and to listen to different points of view, rather than holding on to being right at the expense of our most valuable loving connection. And, as we learn to accept and support our mutual strivings, we find our way toward an ever more satisfying relationship life—and a rich and meaningful inner life too.

HAPPINESS IS AN INSIDE JOB

The idea of "happiness," like the concept of "love," turns up all over the place in literature, in media of all shapes and sizes, even in scripture. It's as elusive as it is ubiquitous; it seems impossible to pin down exactly what it is to be happy, and yet we know it unmistakably when we are. And if we look closely, some patterns emerge. Skiing down a slope after the first snow, looking into a lover's eyes after a night of lovemaking, inventing something that will help others, completing a task that has been long and hard—in all these moments, we know we are part of something that engages our deepest being, in harmony with others, with our environment, and with ourselves.

We also know that we can't sustain happiness by effort; it is capricious and sensitive and by definition exists moment to moment. We don't get there by trying to. In a sense, we don't *get there* at all: as the journalist Sydney Harris wisely observed, "Happiness is a direction, not a place." Eleanor Roosevelt put it another way: "Happiness is not a goal; it is a by-product." We stumble upon it, or it steals up on us, while we're doing other things—such as the work of creating and sustaining love.

In my work with couples, I have found that love and happiness are one and the same when we feel deeply understood and accepted by the ones we love. This does not mean that our partners are somehow responsible for making us happy; just the opposite. Before we can be happy together, we need to be happy within ourselves. My colleague and friend Lisa Cypers Kamen, who is a happiness expert, likes to say that happiness is an inside job, and so, we will see, is love.

Conscious Connection

Susan Johnson writes in her book *The Practice of Emotionally Focused Couple Therapy: Creating Connection* that adult love is "an emotional tie with an irreplaceable other who provides a secure base from which to confront the world and a safe haven, a source of comfort, care, and protection." Building that bond is a complex task—though, ironically, the trick is to do the work it takes to make it simple. It asks us to come to a deep understanding of *who we are* and *who we are with*—to look not just at each other but within ourselves to see the true source of our differences, our longings, and our gifts to each other. In doing this, we're not only building a connection with our own inner life but also communicating this knowledge to those we love, which inevitably leads us toward a deeper and more lasting connection.

An important facet of long-term relationships is the commitment couples make to maintain that connection with each other. Part of what it means to love another person is to accept that we are intimately bound to each other, not only because we have a basic need to be loved and feel connected, but because we have made a commitment to persevere. The deeper our commitment, the greater the likelihood that love will remain alive and vital. Lasting love is made from the concerted effort of two people crafting their own unique relationship from the sweat and toil of daily life and from all the difficulties, conflicts, and hardships that arise in sharing a life together.

Being truly happy together is no simple matter. It requires that we be free from guilt, shame, fear, anxiety, depression and emotional blocks. Can we love in a state of terror or sadness? Can we be happy if we are in conflict with our mate? The obvious answer is "no." To love is to free ourselves, to know something of ourselves, to experience true acceptance—not so easy to produce on demand.

To make love that lasts, we must forge a high-energy emotional bond with the strength to withstand the inevitable storms, then cultivate methods to keep it strong. Knowing how to reprocess a lost connection is an essential skill for keeping love alive. Creating and maintaining an enduring connection takes energy and focus, but the miracle is that love *can* last and become even more satisfying over time.

Equally essential is the ability to form strong attachments in the first place, since from them we build relationships that are safe and secure. Safety and security are the cornerstones of lasting love; they allow us to open up about our secrets, our feelings, and our fears. In a safe and secure relationship, we can find the space to know ourselves and each other in the way that lasting love requires.

Insight and Intimacy

Critical to understanding how intimacy is created and maintained is to accept that it is a function of, and deeply intertwined with, our inner life. True and abiding love requires that we do some soul-searching so we can understand how experience has affected us. It calls for some knowledge about what helps us maintain an intimate connection and what gets in our way. When we appreciate how these sometimes covert processes affect our ability to love, we will be able to work through inevitable disappointments more successfully. When we map the territories below the surface of our psyche, we will be better able to find our way through our personal pain and less likely to dump it on those we love.

Coming to this kind of self-understanding in a relationship requires not only self-reflection but what I call *inter-reflection.* Inter-reflection is the process that lets us see ourselves from behind our lover's eyes. This acquired ability of shifting our perspective to vicariously experience the point of view of the other is at the core of what it means to be intimately connected. It sends a message to our partners that we hear what they are trying to tell us about *their* experience of who *we* are. Expressing and using the insight we gain when we tune in to each other this way is the active process of creating a lasting and loving relationship. Inter-reflection is part of an ongoing dialogue that incorporates the constantly evolving understanding of who we are and who we want to be. Our ability to inter-reflect requires that we trust the insight of our mate and have the desire to know about who we are. Learning to trust in this way, and being open to what we learn, are the building blocks of a solid relationship and the foundation of shared happiness.

The struggle to balance two individual lives and to pay attention to the ebb and flow of moods, feelings, and passions is a challenge, but it's the best way to an enlightened sense of intimacy. The more we're able to be inwardly accepting, the more we're able to be outwardly tolerant. Ultimately, to be happy together each of us must become a better person, one who is worthy of being loved, by being loving and kind ourselves. In this way, a truly committed love relationship brings light into dark places as we discover our true nature in the company of the one we love.

The Cure for What Ails Us

Ever since that morning with Brenna and Jake in my office, I have been investigating the nature of passionate attachments, trying to understand what makes love last. I've observed couples who have forged successful, fulfilling relationships and couples whose relationships have fallen apart. And I've discovered that the couples who make it have several things in common. They understand how negative interactions can break their precious connection to each other. They have made the crucial distinction between how they felt as children and who they are as adults. They grasp how the way they communicate with each other can bring deep feelings to light, and they find ways to handle these feelings that foster an even more intimate connection. They are attuned to each other in a way that allows them to have true empathy. They recognize that the goal of a relationship is to actively create love, not passively receive it.

As I reflect on the experiences of my patients and the qualities that seem to help or hinder them in their work of creating love, I have come to see that true and abiding love—like Eleanor Roosevelt's happiness—is the by-product of loving kindness. Its core components are compassion, understanding, respect, and empathy—because these are the tools we use to develop precious insight into the inner world of our partner and ensure that we're truly happy *together*, as well as the essential steps for resolving conflict when it does arise.

The pain in our relationships may run deep, but we have the cure at our fingertips. Here is how we will heal our wounds—with:

Compassion—for ourselves and for others

Understanding—of where we came from and who we are

Respect—in the way we speak and act

Empathy—toward others and ourselves

The more we are compassionate, the more we will listen with our hearts. The more we are understanding, the better we will know our partner. The more we are respectful, the more we will get respect in return. The more we empathize, the deeper our connection with others and with ourselves. These processes are the essence of inter-reflection, and these are themes that I will come back to throughout the book as we see how the C.U.R.E. works to heal and strengthen relationships at every level. As I say to my patients, if you are not using one of these processes either toward your partner or toward yourself, you are off track.

HOW TO USE THIS BOOK

In the chapters that follow, we'll explore many aspects of relationship, from connection to conflict to commitment, on our way to a fuller understanding of how to be happy together. At the end of each chapter, I'll offer a few questions for you to ask yourself—and, ideally, for you and your partner to ask each other—to open the door to inter-reflection.

- **Chapter 2** opens a discussion about how to create love from everyday life, from pinpointing the places where our painful history may dovetail with our partner's to actively creating a vision for the relationship and a road map for happiness.

- **Chapter 3** explores how myths and fantasies—about family, marriage, rescue, redemption, idealized romance—can both shape our relationships and provide valuable insights into ourselves and others.

- **Chapter 4** defines shame and rage, tracing their roots in our past, explaining how they arise in relationships, and showing how they impact us and our ability to love.

- **Chapter 5** continues the odyssey through the straits and narrows of relationship life by defining true intimacy—that delicate dance between our inner and outer worlds—and exploring ways to cultivate and preserve it.

- **Chapter 6** considers conflict in all its forms, strategies for resolving it, and what we can learn from it to create deeper intimacy.

- **Chapter 7** takes a closer look at creating, repairing, and preserving our precious connection to our partner using such tools as compassionate communication and constructive complaining.

- **Chapter 8** examines the role of sexuality in our relationship life, including the uses of fantasy, the value of monogamy, and the insight sex can give us into who we are, separately and together.

- **Chapter 9** shows how successful couples create the conditions for happiness in their relationships and sums up what it takes to live happily ever after.

Simply put, we get out of relationships what we put into them. Happiness in a relationship is a direct result of deliberate actions that either elevate and intensify feelings or shut them down. We need to be willing to express hard truths, such as how afraid or hurt or unlovable we feel or how we don't trust that love can last. We need to discover the truth within ourselves and then speak it, not to injure but to engage our partner in a process that leads to greater closeness and ever deeper love.

If we are willing to risk opening our hearts and minds, we will find ourselves in a universe that we never knew existed. Binding our heart with another's and finding its strength uncovers what is most precious about life. Love is what gives life its color and fills us with its meaning. It's what keeps us sane and feeds our soul.

Lasting love is liberating and inspiring, and its effects reach far beyond ourselves, extending to our families and communities. Loving couples impact everyone around them; they offer optimism and lead others toward deeper insights about themselves. But most of all, loving relationships infuse us with hope for a more humane society. This book is dedicated to all those who yearn to build a loving relationship that will not only stand the test of time, but will flourish, helping us all live happily together, in the broadest sense, to build a better future and a better world.

2

how love is made

Love never dies a natural death. It dies because we don't know how to replenish its source. It dies of blindness and errors and betrayals. It dies of illness and wounds; it dies of weariness, of witherings, of tarnishings.

—Anaïs Nin

THE WAY A RELATIONSHIP BEGINS is often a far cry from what it's like after many years of being together, and what it's like is what we make it. If our partner asks for help and we don't give it—or if we take a moment to consider our partner's point of view; if we feel entitled to scream obscenities when we're angry—or if we pay close attention to our partner's needs; either way, our actions will have consequences, positive or negative. To ensure that the love we begin with is still there 10 or 20 years in the future is thus a constant process of making and creating a loving environment.

When people talk about the "work" of relationships, what do they mean? Simply that if a relationship is to stay intimate, loving, and happy, it requires some effort on our part. We need to be compassionate and consciously available; to make sure we understand our partner's point of view before we express our own; to speak and act respectfully; to check our defenses at the door and empathize instead of falling into tit-for-tat retaliation. During arguments we must remember who it is we love and what our intentions are for the relationship. At the same time, we must be aware of what is causing our anger, which may mean holding on to it until we do understand it. To find love is a miracle; to keep it takes focus. Relationship is at its core very simple, but simplicity is a complex process.

People have made war in the name of love, spent fortunes in love's pursuit, and even died for love. And although there are many ways of loving—from affectionate friendship, to the infatuation of love at first sight, to the romantic love that arises after infatuation fades, to the consummate connection that is forged in an intimate process over many years—they share a common heart. Diane Ackerman writes in *A Natural History of Love:*

> So it is with love. Values, customs, and protocols may vary from ancient days to the present, but not the majesty of love. People are unique in the way they walk, dress, and gesture, yet we're able to look at two people—one wearing a business suit, the other a sarong—and recognize that both of them are clothed. Love also has many fashions, some bizarre and (to our taste) shocking, others more familiar, but all are part of a phantasmagoria we know. In the Serengeti of the heart, time and nation are irrelevant. On that plain all fires are the same fire.

Others have recognized that fire, too, and given it names of their own. Pioneer psychologist Harry Stack Sullivan wrote that love is the state in which the needs and feelings of the other are as important as or more important than our own. Jean-Paul Sartre wrote of love as a wish or call for the other to come out. Sigmund Freud is well known for describing the two most important conditions in life as love and work. Milan Kundera describes love as interrogation. These notions of love all have a common theme: an intense feeling that pulls one's thoughts and desires toward the loved one.

For many of us, that intense pull is the defining characteristic of a romantic relationship—and the thing that makes *being* in love so irresistible to us. We think of romance as the stuff of grand gestures, selfless acts, and consuming feelings of *till death do us part.* We yearn to be filled with the contentment that the thought of love conjures up. But real love is more than romantic thoughts and feelings passively received. Real love is actively made, and we must consciously choose to make it, not just once but throughout our lives together, over and over again.

LOVE IN THE MAKING

When Jeri-Ann and Josh came to see me, I could see that they were locked in a negative cycle. Their interactions seemed to consist mostly of angrily criticizing each other. Jeri-Ann berated her husband for never making plans to go out, never bringing her flowers, and never helping her around the house as a way for them to spend time together on the weekends. He sat quietly shaking his head, feeling hurt by the criticism.

I said to her, "I think you are actually saying something quite romantic." She looked at me quizzically. I explained that everything she was pointing out in a negative way was also about her sense of what she wanted from a loving relationship. I repeated back to her in positive language what she was asking Josh for: "Josh, I wish you could see that my anger is really about how hurt I feel when I don't think you want to spend time with me. What really makes me feel loved by you is when you bring me flowers or write a note to me telling me that you love me. I know that you do love me, but I think that sometimes you have difficulty expressing it." She wanted love and support, but her romantic message was tucked away beneath her criticism, because she didn't feel safe enough to express her deepest romantic feelings directly.

Jeri-Ann and Josh both acknowledged that this rang true. She was so afraid her husband didn't share her feelings that she couldn't risk being positive and vulnerable. And when he felt criticized, he became defensive and then withdrew.

The rest of the session went differently. As he understood the feelings that lay beneath her criticism, he was much more willing to respond lovingly. We went on to discuss all the activities that created more love between them, and we agreed that they needed to continue to talk about what loving meant to each other and how best to express it.

Walking the Talk

Jeri-Ann and Josh were learning to talk to each other in the truest language of love: not sweet nothings (though these have their place), but talk that is romantic precisely because it's realistic. Such a reality-based romantic dialogue might start something like, "When you talk to me about what you want and things that you are thinking about doing, especially when it includes me, it makes me love you more." The response might be, "Yes, I want you to know what I'm thinking and how important you are to every decision I make."

I saw this kind of reality-based romantic talk in action during a discussion with Dan and Kim, a couple making wedding plans. Kim was having problems with her wedding planner and it looked as if she wouldn't be able to get the job done in time. She complained about her frustration to Dan, and he in turn blamed her for the slow progress. Their typical way of reacting to this kind of problem was to reenact their family processes, which involved Kim flying into a defensive tirade in response to Dan's angry attacks. After the initial distance this created, they would recover, but the next time the issue came up, they would go through the same cycle with the same result.

This time, after understanding their family patterns in therapy and some work on mutual realizations about how they were behaving as their parents had with them, they worked at having a different experience. Dan decided to take over the responsibility of dealing with the wedding planner for his fiancée. He had been afraid to take control for fear of doing it wrong and being criticized. He took a risk. At our next session Kim turned to him with tears in her eyes and said that this was the first time in her life that she felt truly supported and loved. When she was a child, her father used to criticize her for not being what he thought she should be at every turn. So when Dan criticized her she would go on the defensive and attack him. Now, instead, she felt more love for him. He had seized the opportunity to be supportive and helpful, and at that critical moment he actively created more love. Every relationship has moments like these where we can create more love by our actions.

This short vignette illustrates one of the central concepts of creating love. It is a conscious choice emanating from a deep understanding of our own and our partner's needs and feelings. Often, this requires us to act counterintuitively: in this case, Dan had to do something different from what he had always done and what had always been done to him. It's not necessarily smooth or seamless to go against our internal grain, but when our intention is to create more love, we then will be more likely to focus our attention on what we need to do to make it so. If we can stop for a moment and think about what our partner needs and try to respond—while still being aware of our own feelings—we will often be rewarded with a loving response. Here, Dan took the opportunity to create more love by doing something that he knew his fiancée needed. She had never experienced someone supporting her in this way. They went on to have a fabulous wedding.

Exploring the Ecosystem

If we have experienced pain around needing support, as Kim had, we may have difficulty accepting it when it is offered. Then our natural state will be to defend against fearful, vulnerable feelings and automatically respond in that defensive way. Even when we think we're doing the right thing in an intimate relationship—and think we know what the "right thing" is—there are often hidden processes just below the surface that can complicate matters at a moment's notice. So how can we continue loving our mate without projecting our own inner struggles onto him or her?

Love is sensitive to all exchanges between people. The interaction of wants, needs, desires, and personal pain forms the ecosystem that we and our loved one inhabit, both externally (between us as a couple) and internally (within ourselves). Difficulties in loving our mate arise from both the internal processes that govern our behavior and the defenses that spill into our relationship. The more pain we're in, the more our defenses will try to push it out and therefore onto our partner. Clearly, the more we know about these processes and defenses, the better we will be at limiting their impact on our loved ones. This is what it means to create love from the inside out.

Communicating our internal dialogue is the best chance we have for sustaining a loving relationship. Bringing feelings, complaints, hurts, and misunderstandings to the surface, and working through them if need be, is the *major* activity for creating love; it is what keeps the ecosystem in balance and allows it to thrive. Our worst fear is that exposing our pain, expressing needs, and allowing our feelings to be known will bring criticism, humiliation, or abandonment—but the opposite is usually true. *Not* expressing needs, wants, and feelings is more likely to cause rejection or, at the very least, alienation from our partner. When there are many unresolved issues between people, it creates distance and interrupts their ability to feel loving toward each other. But talking about what we are experiencing is a way to connect. As we learn to talk about our pain, our fears, and our hurt feelings, we build a stronger intimacy.

Then why is talking to one another so difficult to do? The trouble is, most people go about expressing themselves by simply using what they know, and many times this knowledge fails them. More understanding is required. We must comprehend not only what happens inside us when we feel criticized, rejected, or judged, but also what is happening inside our partner, and be able to factor that knowledge into our conversation, especially during conflicts. The mixture of emotions, thoughts, shame, guilt, infantile longings, and painful experiences from both sides can be quite difficult to unravel and clarify. There is all the more need to be calm, thoughtful, and responsive during these times. Clearing away what complicates love—and making space for the tender acceptance of the other and the development of skills and behavior that support a strong connection—is an essential part of what it means to love over time. For sure, this is no easy task, but in the chapters ahead we will go through all the necessary steps to create constructive dialogue.

THE FOUNDATION FOR LOVE

To be happy together, we need to build and maintain loving connections with our partner. The stronger these connections are, the more lasting our love will be. Love and romance are nurtured as much by small, everyday things as by grand gestures—and sometimes more so. A patient recently explained to me that he had taken his wife on many wonderful vacations, so he couldn't understand why she complained about feeling unloved. But listening to her, we found that it was his condescending attitude, controlling behavior, and constant anger that made her feel so bad. So it didn't matter what he did; his behavior took away all the love he intended for her.

Here are some basic building blocks for loving connection—concepts to work with as a couple in your everyday world.

- **Boundaries**: Understanding what is acceptable and what is not is vital for love to grow. We need to take time to outline what our boundaries are so we can live within them. Boundaries are created by our feelings about what does or doesn't feel good.

- **Consideration**: To be considerate about the things that are important to your mate is essential for harmony. Helping out, remembering important events and agreements, and doing things your partner wants are small gestures that can have a large effect over time.

- **Fairness**: Being fair helps keep a relationship balanced. Sharing household chores, vacations, spending, friends, and responsibilities toward relatives creates more harmony and positive feelings.

- **Tolerance**: Our ability to tolerate our partner's foibles and flaws is important for lasting peace. Tolerance for differences in feelings, ways of doing things, parenting styles, and the other opposing views that all couples have is a key component of creating love.

- **Responsibility**: Being able to own our part of a problem is essential for conflict resolution. One of the main reasons for divorce is the inability of one partner or the other to accept responsibility for difficulties in the relationship.

- **Support**: Support takes many forms, from helping your partner fulfill dreams and aspirations to providing care when he or she is sick or defeated. It sends a message that you believe in your partner and you are on his or her side.

- **Making time for sex or affection or both:** When couples actively create space and time for sex and affection, they will feel more contented more of the time. Physical and emotional contentment is what supports monogamy.

- **The ability to bear ambivalence:** This is the act of staying even when everything in you wants to split. Being angry, turned off, and ready to run, yet staying, listening, and fighting hard during tough times is an essential skill for long-term relationships.

Roadblocks to Love

Just as there are methods and means for creating love, there are defensive processes that can obstruct it. Let's take a look at some of the main love-killers.

- **Globalization:** "Everybody does that." Globalization essentially obscures the truth. If someone doesn't want to admit that he or she has some responsibility in the problem, globalization is a perfect distraction.

- **Blame-shifting:** "And you do the same thing but worse." Another excellent way to shift the blame away from yourself and back onto the other person.

- **Victimhood:** "I'm so good to you, and you treat me so badly." The victim is always innocent and good. This is an emotional double whammy. "Not only are you picking on me but you should feel guilty because I am so good."

- **Gaslighting:** "I was just kidding; can't you take a joke?" "Noise? What noise?" This process is more insidious because it is an effort to make the other person feel crazy in order to gain power and control.

- **Entitlement:** "You're the one who made me angry. You deserve it." Entitlement is like a free pass to behave however you want to because you are the aggrieved party. This kind of behavior is a surefire defense because nothing gets through.

- **Denial:** "I'm not angry." Denial is an emotional way to slam the door on any form of communication about what went wrong.

- **Displacement:** "Just because you had a bad day at work, don't take it out on me." Displacement happens more than most people know or understand. It's important to tell our partner when we think this is going on.

- **Guilt:** "I work my ass off to give you everything and you can't even make me some tea." Guilt is often part of playing the victim, but it can also be used as a control mechanism.

- **Shame/Blame:** "You're a human slug. You never do anything." This process is essentially infantile because there is no empathy or compassion in it. Infants and children are not expected to be compassionate, but adults are.

- **Stonewalling:** "This is the way I am; take it or leave it." Stonewalling is exactly that: it shuts down communication. Another form of stonewalling is simply to say nothing.

- **Projection:** "You think I'm stupid, don't you?" This process is very common because most people are not in touch with how insecure they feel, so what they experience feels like it is coming from the other person when it is really coming from within.

- **Devaluation:** "You really could lose some of that extra weight." Devaluation is a defense against caring and needing anyone. The less others mean to us, the less we need them.

Constructive Communicating

As we look at what it takes to sustain a loving relationship, it may appear to be quite daunting. I try to support couples by explaining that if they can learn effective problem solving, it will only be difficult in the beginning. If we can evaluate and understand what causes negative communication, both from our own assessment and from listening to what our partner is telling us, our reality will, in time, meet our expectations. We may go many months or even years between serious conflicts once we know how to create a loving environment that is rich with humor and loving kindness.

Learning to evaluate the way we're communicating, and to talk to our partner in constructive new ways, can be a challenge in itself, especially if the old ways are deeply ingrained. So I work with couples to help them change their interactive style and incorporate the elements of effective communication. Effective communication involves our ability to recognize what it is that we are feeling, then what it is we want. In this process, we take time to initially assess what is wrong or what we need to communicate. Next, we make sure that the other person gets the message the way we are intending it. Then we recognize and express what the problem or the need is. Once we have defined the problem or the need, we can then look at possible solutions that both people feel comfortable with. Most important in this process is to listen with empathy, tolerance for differences, and understanding about what is being said, and to provide feedback to show that we recognize each other's positions. The dialogue below contains most of the elements of effective problem solving. This may look easy, but guess what, it's not.

He: When you withdraw, it scares me. My parents withdrew from me when I didn't behave the way they wanted, and my girlfriends rejected me because I didn't behave the way they wanted, so when I get angry or upset with you I'm afraid to show it because I'm afraid that you'll throw me away. So I push *you* away.

She: I will never throw you away because you get mad at me, but I will get upset if you don't tell me what's bothering you. It always comes out anyway. We have to tell each other how we feel without tearing away our love for each other. When I say something that is insensitive and you shut down, and then I get more angry and critical, we are just repeating our old patterns. How can we make this different?

He: We could start by understanding what we are doing to alienate each other. Then we could take some time to find out what we are after. Once we know, then we can help each other to give what we need and want.

The key elements here are support, understanding, and a willingness to reflect on one's own behavior. Using self-knowledge and feelings to resolve conflicts together creates a compassionate and loving outcome. The more a couple can create these kinds of conversations, the better they will be at creating love that lasts.

THE ROOTS OF CONFLICT

To truly understand what healthy communication is all about, we need to consider the complexity of what may be causing conflicts with our mate. An argument about putting the cap back on the toothpaste may actually contain clues to buried feelings. The core of the conflict may be a sense of feeling invisible or needing to control, but the cap is the way our feelings are ignited, so the toothpaste is where the argument is focused. Many couples scratch their heads and wonder how such an innocuous comment ("You never put the cap back on") could lead to such a big fight. The answer lies in the channel that the toothpaste opens into each person's life history and personal issues. Of course there are times when it is just about the toothpaste. The trick is to know the difference.

When we fall in love, we have only a limited knowledge of our partner; we haven't yet been through difficulties, losses, and stressful situations together. Over the years, the everyday routines and the vagaries of existence will bring out all aspects of our personalities—good and bad—and our personal issues along with them. There are the usual mundane relationship conflicts, time conflicts, energy-level conflicts, temperature conflicts, television, music, food, and value conflicts that happen in the normal course of living. There are also major stresses such as job loss, death in the family, illness, depression, and losses due to gambling, drugs, or extramarital affairs. These circumstances throw relationships into crisis that many couples are unprepared for and do not have the skills to work through together. Such problems have complexities that make them difficult to work through even in a very healthy marriage where both partners have good problem-solving skills; many less healthy relationships will fail under this pressure.

How we handle daily conflicts relates not only to our partner but to our relationship with ourselves. If we feel that every disagreement is a signal that we are bad or unlovable—or if we're convinced that our side of the conflict is the right and only way—then we're adding to the trouble we are already in. If we are flooded with shame, guilt, or rage when a conflict arises, we will have great difficulty separating our internal conflict from our relationship conflict. If our family process was to attack or defend, we will mimic that response during relationship struggles because it's what we know. People with unresolved internal conflicts are prone to be defensive whenever there is a sense that they have done something wrong.

Conflict from Within

Let's examine some ways in which unresolved personal issues get externalized in relationship conflicts.

- **Being uncomfortable in one's own skin:** When we feel this way, we believe we must hide our true self from our partner. This creates distance and ultimately distrust.

- **Negatively comparing ourselves to others, or envy:** Negatively comparing ourselves to our partner because we envy him or her will cause us to become competitive, especially if we are not aware that we feel that way. Envy is the outcome of feeling less than others, and it makes us defensive and competitive. It's painful to feel that others have something that we don't have and will never have and that they have it because they are superior or we are inferior. So, we may try to tear the other person down to feel better. We can do this in several ways: passively, by not listening or not showing up or not keeping our agreements and then criticizing our partner for being angry; or actively, by trying to one-up our partner or put him or her down with sarcasm.

- **Self-critical feelings:** These emanate from perfectionism or idealism. Either way, we become critical of our partner.

- **Idealized expectations of oneself and others:** Having overly romantic ideals creates disappointment and causes a sense of failure within the relationship and disconnection from our partner. For example, if our partner expects us to be loving all the time and always be thinking of little ways to express love, it may be very disappointing when that doesn't happen.

- **Feeling disorganized and confused:** When we are unable to carry our part of the load, we overburden our partner, which leads to resentment and loss of respect.

- **Fear of failure or success:** Fear of success is actually the fear of failure turned upside-down. One dysfunctional member of a relationship can make the relationship dysfunctional. For example, if one person is successful and the other is afraid of success and won't try to do well, it creates a depression in the relationship and skews the power dynamic in favor of the successful partner, which can create envy, anger, distance, and withdrawal.

- **Feeling depressed and anxious throughout the day:** This can cause the whole relationship to be anxious and depressed.

- **Feeling like a victim:** This is a subtle form of punishment that makes the other person angry and causes him or her to pull away or punish in return. This causes resentment and loss of respect.

- **Perfectionism:** This serves to make the other person feel criticized or inferior.

- **Helplessness:** Feelings of powerlessness and passivity create distance and inertia.

- **Feeling weak and worthless:** Our mind automatically hides these feelings from our awareness, and if we don't recognize them, they will ultimately disconnect us from our mate.

- **Feeling blocked or frozen:** This is a sign of depression within the relationship, and it keeps the relationship from moving forward.

Recognition and Resolution

When we find ourselves in a fight that cycles around and around, it's a dead giveaway that something deeper is going on—often, that one of these internal conflicts is making itself externally felt. When an argument seems locked in a negative cycle, it helps to take it down a few levels to find out what is causing the hurt or creating the anger. It is important to understand that we may need something we are not getting—or be getting something that we don't want or that hurts us. The endless cycle is created because people tend to stay on the surface and get locked into a who-said-what or who's-right-or-wrong pattern that doesn't address the principal concern. Recognizing where we're really hurting is the first step toward working the conflict through.

Because at the heart of many conflicts is a completely different set of feelings from the feelings being played out on the surface, we may feel hurt by our partner but not know what is hurting us. If our mate thinks it's a good joke to tell us that we are a "loser" or what we just did was "stupid," we may not see the humor in those statements if we also happen to believe that we are either a loser or stupid. Importantly, if we know this about ourselves and are able to see clearly that we are neither a loser nor stupid, but instead that our reaction is the outcome of some bad experience, we may eventually be able to see the humor in our partner's remarks—or be able to ask politely that he or she not use those words to talk about who we are, even in jest.

One of the most important processes in coming to a clear idea of what we are responding to internally is to know ourselves well. If we can see our negative self feelings (like feeling unlovable or as though we are worth less than our partner), and then understand where these personal myths came from in our past, we will be less likely to project them onto our partner in a conflict. We also need to determine where the negative feelings are coming from. Once we are clear about the origin of the problem, we can make better choices about what we need to say. This new perspective, derived from our understanding of ourselves and our partner, can move us toward compromise, reconciliation, and a fresh approach to the conflict. Resolution must include mutual respect, tolerance for differences, and a willingness to listen to those differences with an open mind. Let me say again that the goal of all conflict resolution should be that we feel closer to each other, so that the outcome and the process of resolution is always constructive.

When a conflict turns nasty, it may take a long time for loving feelings to return—if they ever do. It's difficult enough to be vulnerable and open up to each other under the best of circumstances; in an environment that feels unsafe, it becomes nearly impossible. By handling our conflicts with care, concern, interest, and empathy—which means taking a step back, considering what our feelings mean, and then being able to articulate what is bothering us or what we need or don't need—we are doing the best we can to steer clear of alienating our partner and instead are actively preserving our emotional connection.

THE CONFLUENCE OF PAIN

Not surprisingly, what's hurting us in a relationship today is often rooted much earlier in our life, in painful experiences that intertwine with our partner's to wound us in ways we may not at first understand. Phil and Donna are a prime example. Though they were very happy to find each other—both had spent many years alone and wanted a relationship—conflict soon became their main mode of connection as they cycled between attacking each other and making up. In fact, their decision to get married came from feeling especially connected after one of their most dramatic fights. Conflict was all they knew about being intimate.

Their conflicts grew out of a series of negative and insulting remarks over small misunderstandings. Phil would mentally make a list of complaints about Donna and withdraw into righteous indignation. When he finally whipped out the list, they would fight about it for days, ending up in a heap of frustration that would eventually lead to make-up sex. They were locked in an emotional prison of their own making.

Donna had custody of her son from a previous marriage, and Phil had joint custody of a daughter with his former wife. In the first year of their marriage, Phil lost his job. No longer able to retreat into work, or to his separate home as he had before they married, he became depressed. At the same time, Donna began to rise within her company and loved every minute of it. She had always relied on men to support her; now she was financially independent for the first time in her life. As the months stretched on, the tension became unbearable, and they fought bitterly. Phil, feeling rejected, openly criticized Donna in front of the children. He would sometimes punish her by withdrawing and refusing to speak to her. When he did open up, he raged at her with all the vitriol he could muster, and she gave it right back.

When they came to me, their pattern was well established. To see what lay behind their present pain, I asked them to tell me more about their past. Phil, I learned, had come from an authoritarian household. His father was a tough street kid who came up the hard way, fighting all the way up the corporate ladder. He trained Phil to be strong, never cry, and never run from a fight. Phil and his father fought throughout his childhood and adolescence. His mother, meanwhile, frequently lamented to her son the plight she was in and complained of being a slave to his father. Phil identified with both of them: from his father he adopted an authoritarian, aggressive personality, and from his mother he learned to be the victim. From that position, as the aggrieved party, he felt entitled to punish Donna. Phil had a quiet charm that impressed people, but when he was angry, withdrawn, and self-pitying, he was impossible to reach.

Donna had grown up in a poor family with an alcoholic father and an overburdened mother. Her father was distant and unavailable except when he was engaging her in heated and passionate conflicts concerning daily chores and other things that she would forget to do. Donna learned to fend for herself throughout her childhood, but after adolescence, she enlisted men to take care of her, especially financially. When she was able to find a good job, her newfound freedom thrilled her, but it also opened up her resentment toward men. When Phil lost his job, Donna lost her husband as the breadwinner and, along with it, her respect for him; she felt abandoned again, and her anger toward her abandoning father resurfaced in her present relationship. She vowed to herself that she would never again be controlled by a man. Her anger and distrust caused her to hold in her feelings and complaints, so when Phil became aggressive and critical, she would reject him with a cold indifference that cut him deeply. Phil would boil over into a full-blown rage and then withdraw into being a victim.

Playing out the pain of the past, unable to connect in the present, with no idea how to communicate their needs and wants to each other, Phil and Donna alternated between hopelessness and fruitless attempts at reconciliation. How were they to get out of this mess?

When Wounds Collide

Working with couples and hearing their stories gives me a bird's-eye view of how we experience relationships throughout our lives. What I often observe with couples in conflict is something I call the *confluence of pain*—a place where each person's wounds from his or her own experiences collide with the other person's. In fact, this is the central cause of most couple conflicts: the way each person's pain reacts with the pain of his or her partner.

Personal wounds are created from our reaction to being abused either by our caregivers early on in life or by others along the way. If we were criticized, rejected, physically beaten, sexually abused, neglected, or abandoned, these experiences will generate pain no matter when they occur. This pain forms into emotional wounds so sensitive that if anyone "touches" them—say, by being critical or abusive or neglectful—our defenses are quickly marshaled for protection. Typical defenses to personal pain include deflection, shutting down, withdrawal, and angry outbursts. Couples who experience intense conflict are often responding to the confluence of their personal pain generated from each one's emotional wounds. Each person's pain flows into the other's, creating a combustible mix.

If a woman felt as a child that she was not interesting to her father, and then marries a man who has trouble expressing his feelings because he was punished for having them, his reticence may bring the rejection she felt from her father vividly back to her. If one partner grew up never feeling valued and the other grew up experiencing constant criticism and coldness, they will mutually fly into an orbit of anger when either one experiences criticism or withdrawal. Or say one person felt invisible and the other abandoned: now, when the first one feels invisible, she withdraws, which makes the other one feel abandoned. In some couples, requests for affection and reassurance may be met with resistance, which will reopen old wounds into fresh pain that gets converted into anger and other defenses that can alienate the other person still more.

In each instance, conflicts—and new wounds—arise from the confluence of pain. This is why self-knowledge is so critical to lasting love. If we are unaware of the nature and origin of our wounds, we will also be clueless as to the way these wounds function as defenses.

Finding a Way Out

So how *did* Donna and Phil get out of the mess they were in? As we worked together, they began to see that their worst difficulties arose from their own confluence of pain—Donna's anger at abandonment, Phil's aggrieved withdrawal—and to grasp that they were operating on antiquated principles that were tearing away at the fabric of their relationship. Now they could work on understanding their negative process and learning to communicate effectively.

The first order of business was to debunk their idealized, romantic fantasy of what the relationship "should be." Then we looked into family issues to understand how they were being played out in the current situation. They learned more about what was hurting them and what they were trying to communicate through their hurt feelings and entitlement to rage. As they were able to look, see, and understand where their pain was coming from and what had originally caused it, they were much more able to identify the feelings when they started to enter into a conflict and back off before it escalated. They learned how to develop their own unique vocabulary for how their issues were colliding, and they worked out a way to stop one another, soothe one another, and organize the conflict around solutions that were emotionally based. Donna could say to Phil, at the opening of a conversation that she knew would bring up his issues, something like: "I want to talk to you about something, but I don't want you to take it personally because I don't mean it that way. It is just that my feelings are hurt and I know that that's my issue."

Importantly, they made agreements about what they needed to do to make the relationship work for each of them, like taking time-outs and talking about how they felt instead of blaming. Because they loved each other and wanted the relationship, they stuck to those agreements. They also worked on communicating their wishes for the future—including the *immediate* future with simple requests such as "When you take a shower, could you please remember to hang up the towels afterwards because it's important to me?" They worked on responding with active listening skills: "I hear what you're saying, that it makes you feel that I care about your needs when I pick up after myself." They learned more about compromise, the importance of empathy, and the need to express complaints without criticizing or blaming. They learned clear new ways to articulate their deeper feelings and concerns.

THE RELATIONSHIP ETHIC

What Phil and Donna needed, above all, was to talk openly about what kind of life they wanted with each other and what they needed to do to make that happen. As they moved in this direction, learning to engage in real dialogue and work together to resolve problems, they were creating a new *relationship ethic,* a vision for the relationship that both of them could live with and believe in.

The relationship ethic gives couples a set of principles that they can live by—a guide to actively creating happiness that they can refer to anywhere along their way. The ethic that Phil and Donna fashioned was unlike any other but contained what was important to each of them, including agreements about how to communicate hurt feelings and needs. It also served as a code of conduct—a set of standards to guide their behavior toward each other and within themselves. An ethical principle for our relationship could look something like: *We promise to not raise our voices to each other, we will not swear, call each other names, refer to family members or friends during an argument, bring up the past, or use sensitive material we have previously shared as a means of hurting each other. We promise to come back to the table and talk things out when we have an argument.* These statements form a relationship ethic that couples live with and can remind each other of during difficult moments. Such an ethic is a guidepost, a set of principles that are agreed to and offer a road map to important behaviors that set the tone for a more stable and loving relationship.

Writing Our Own Code

Moral codes and ethics help move us toward relationship well-being. Moral development provides the structure that guides our behavior. Lawrence Kohlberg, the renowned developmental psychologist, created a paradigm for moral development based on the belief that moral codes are active developmental processes. He defined a hierarchy of stages in our moral learning over time, beginning in childhood. From ages 3 to 12 we behave according to what our parents believe is right and wrong; then we behave in ways that fit with what others believe is right and wrong during adolescence and early adulthood. In the next stage, adulthood, beginning at around 21, we take our cues from what the larger society believes is correct in an effort to fit in with our culture and what our peers have agreed is conventional wisdom. At some point, depending on our interest and our personal quest for meaning in our lives, we may reach the highest level of moral development, according to Kohlberg, when we form our own moral code by internalizing our personal and moral beliefs. To him, true moral maturity is reached when we must face ourselves as the final moral arbiter for our behavior. To not be ashamed of ourselves is then our highest moral value. In relationships, developing a moral and ethical code of behavior is the most evolved form of loving.

The motion picture *High Noon*, starring Gary Cooper and Grace Kelly, tells the story of a small-town marshal who stuck to his moral code in the face of mighty opposition from his wife and the entire town. The townsfolk were more concerned about saving themselves than standing up to a gang of outlaws bent on destruction. The marshal becomes a heroic figure because he decides that his moral and ethical code requires him to be true to his oath of office and do his job by standing up to the gang. His ethical code of conduct is more important than everyone, even his wife, turning against him. He could not live with himself if he didn't fight the injustice.

For couples who want to do the work to develop their moral and ethical codes, there are many things to consider along the way. We can ask each other about suffering in our past and what this means to the future of our relationship. We can ask: What is it that feels best when we get it? What is it that we deeply wish for from our loved ones? What do we dream about and are afraid to tell anyone for fear we'll be laughed at? Can we be so kind, so understanding, and so able to let things go that we can find a way into each other's hearts, knowing that each of us will take tender care of that privilege?

Other ethical codes might contain thoughts about fidelity, support for one another's sexual needs, and the value of making a connection before sex. They might be based on the moral obligation to be truly friends to one another, loyal, truthful, helpful, and on each other's side. If those agreements are broken, we are held accountable.

A Code for Creating Love

For couples, the development of moral processes and belief systems helps relationships run more smoothly and provides an important steadying influence. To develop our moral code we must question, scrutinize, evaluate, and enunciate those values we hold to be important. These earnest efforts to create shared values are the bulwark of relationship stability. Establishing values we agree upon is like reaching level ground where a relationship can find its balance and keep moving forward.

Lasting love is supported best by principles, opinions, feelings, ethics, and morals that represent what is important to both people—

and that both people are willing to make a priority. As I sit with couples who are fighting about an issue that seems so crucial at the time, I often say, "What's more important, your relationship or being right?" They usually stop fighting, because what I am saying rings true. They see that they've gotten lost in their own hurt, in being self-righteous, in trying to win. When writing a code for a relationship, we can set rules of engagement, like how to show respect and concern

Some Values That Serve Love

As we begin the process of creating our own values, there are some truths that support that process. Here are some of them.

• Loving and caring trumps everything else.

• Your relationship comes before being right.

• Listening is the highest value.

• Anger is natural yet counterproductive.

• Yelling, hitting below the belt, swearing, or name-calling is not problem solving.

• Blame, shame, and criticism create distance and resentment.

• Taking statements personally disconnects us from our partner and closes us within ourselves.

• Never assume. Always check out what you think before you assume it's true.

• Be willing to look at yourself from the perspective of the other person.

during discussions and how to include different points of view, that help keep our viewpoints from diverging into conflict.

AT PEACE WITH OURSELVES

Love over time grows from understanding two things: how we have been shaped by our life experience, and how we interact with our partner in regard to his or her feelings and needs. To put it another way, lasting love arises from a deep knowledge and acceptance of *who we are* and *who we are with.* Only when we come to this knowledge—and accept, even forgive, the wrongs of our past—can we take responsibility for the outcome of our own lives. We cease blaming others for our misfortunes and clear a space where love can thrive.

Melanie Klein, who worked closely with Sigmund Freud and contributed many classic works to the field of psychology, wrote:

> A good relation to ourselves is a condition for love, tolerance and wisdom towards others. This good relation to ourselves has . . . developed in part from a friendly, loving and understanding attitude towards other people, namely, those who meant much to us in the past, and our relationship to whom has become part of our minds and personalities. If we have become able, deep in our unconscious minds, to clear our feelings to some extent towards our parents of grievances, and have forgiven them for the frustrations we had to bear, then we can be at peace with ourselves and are able to love others in the true sense of the word.

The words of Melanie Klein ring as true now as when she wrote them so many decades ago. She goes on to say that:

> Part of the process of loving someone is to make peace with ourselves, our history, and our upbringing. To find those

inevitable similarities and differences is the beginning stage of relating to another person without losing who we are and what is truly essential about us. How love is made not only involves how we behave towards our partner but how we are towards ourselves. How can we love someone else when we have no love to give?

When we can weave together what we need to do for ourselves with what we need to give to and get from our partner, we create a richer, more satisfying, and ultimately more contented life. What we need to do for ourselves is to create our own self-esteem, advance in our work or career, and take care of our health and our personal issues. What we need to give to and get from our partner is love, affection, comfort, support, sex, and companionship. When successfully married couples are asked the secret of their success, invariably they answer, "It takes work." It does take work, but we must remember that it is love's work, and when we give ourselves to it we are rewarded with sweet serenity and a sense that love will last because we make it so. We make love last when we create a vision for our relationship that we live by and we do the work of sticking to our promises. Then we know we can reach out to each other in difficult times and help each other and be good to each other, happy together as the years go by.

Falling in love is a mystery, but loving that same person over a lifetime is the ultimate personal challenge. For love to last, vital elements need to come together: an ongoing sex life, a satisfying lifestyle, the ability to connect deeply through compassionate honesty, even just working out a way to get through daily life. Lasting love requires that each person be fully committed and willing to do the work that produces an emotional connection. Both partners must feel safe and secure, so that they can express themselves without judgment or criticism. Their daily conversation must contain active compassion, empathy, understanding, and kindness.

For Your Inter-Reflection

How Love Is Made

1. What do you like about your relationship? When you are the most happy with your partner, what is he or she doing?

2. What would you like to change about your relationship? When you are the *least* happy with your partner, what is he or she doing?

3. Can you identify the confluence of pain in your relationship?

4. What about your relationship would you like to be different from the way you grew up?

5. Try writing an ethical code for your relationship. Ask your partner to do the same, then share your thoughts. Work toward agreeing on the principles that you feel are essential to maintain peace and harmony in your relationship.

6. Make a wish list for your future together.

myth, fantasy, and reality

*It is easy to imagine fantasy as physical and myth as real. We do
it almost every moment. We do this as we dream, as we think,
and as we cope with the world about us. But these worlds of
fantasy that we form into the solid things around us are the source
of our discontent. They inspire our search to find ourselves.*

— Evan Walker

A LOVE SONG SWELLS ON THE RADIO, romantic memories flood our
senses, and fantasies fill our hearts with renewed desire for a loved
one. We're responding to the primal pull of romantic myth—a force
as old as human history, changing according to the specific needs
and mores of each age.

For many centuries, love was the province of the upper classes, who
had the freedom to ponder love because they were far away from the
struggle to survive. Aristocrats immersed themselves in the drama and
passion of love's vicissitudes. It was fashionable in 18th-century France,
for example, to embrace, and dramatize through poetry, fiction, and
theater, the intensity of idealistic or unrequited love. By the 20th
century, romantic love had blossomed into an equal-opportunity
cultural phenomenon, in a process intensified and heavily influenced
by media and advertising. Today, romance is big business, and ads for

diamonds, cars, clothing, even air fresheners fuel our national obsession with romantic love. Television, film, and popular music have also made hay out of romance. They especially play on the myth that there is one perfect love that will cure all our ills—making it the centerpiece of our hopes and dreams. This fantasy—that to find "the one" will somehow transform our lives into happily-ever-after scenarios—is such a staple of modern life that it has become an end in itself. The underlying message is that love is curative and does not require any work itself.

As we saw in the last chapter, real love is not just the stuff of romantic dreams. But myth and fantasy can provide important insights into our inner life. Understanding how they affect the way we love is a critical component of the quest to love more deeply.

THE MAKING OF MYTH, THE FUNCTION OF FANTASY

There are several ways to understand how myth and fantasy function and inform us about our inner workings. They can, if understood properly, enlighten us about what we want and need from each other. They allow us to enter a world of possibilities that can deepen our loving process. And they help us to understand how we create expectations that challenge our ability to love. If we place these two different and yet related phenomena into their proper perspective, myth and fantasy can give us important information about what we believe, who we are, how we want to be with others, and how we want them to be with us.

Explaining the Universe

Myths, at their most basic, are attempts to make sense of things around us or respond to an external event by making sense of it within us. They contain both cultural and psychological information. Cultural myths originally sprang from oral tradition, which was a means of passing important concepts and values on to younger generations before print was available. Myths sought to teach, inspire, and explain what seemed mysterious: the heavens, the tides, time, the seasons, the origin of life, how the sun crossed the sky, and why bad things happened.

As myths were replaced by science and humans learned more and more about how things worked, ancient explanatory myths largely disappeared. Modern myths are focused more on explaining how and what love means, as in the myth of "happily ever after," or the notion that we each have only "one true love," or the idea of an inescapable fate or destiny. Myths can overlap with fantasy or even other myths. A psychological myth might include a fantasy that if we can attain perfection then we will attract that one special love, or it may be overlapped by a personal myth that we are unlovable and a redemptive myth providing hope that true love can cure us. Personal myths are about who we think we are as opposed to who we actually are.

Personal myths about ourselves can be both reality-based and completely off-kilter. We may imagine ourselves to be perfect or selfless when we're neither. When we attempt to find the truth about ourselves or our relationship, we may need to tussle with the differences between our myths and our reality. We'll look more closely at how to do this a little later in the chapter.

The Waking Dream

Fantasies function differently than myths because they occur entirely *within* us, whereas myths can be a part of the broader culture. Our fantasy life often stems from deeply held wishes, hopes, dreams, and romantic or sexual desires. Fantasies may also include negative images in response to rage, rejection, or shame and can produce revenge and/or redemptive fantasies. Fantasies can function like defenses, helping both to protect us from pain and to extinguish it. For example, we may respond to being rejected by a loved one with violent fantasies that both defend against our worst fear that we are unlovable and fill our minds with negative images that release bad feelings.

Because fantasies can be negative or positive, they may fill our heads with images throughout the day. We may see someone across the room or walking down the street and fantasize that this person will save us, make us happy, or be the perfect sexual partner. Our fantasies may go wild, fueling our longing for liberation from loneliness, filling us with hope, excitement, wishes, or desires. But desires for what, exactly? That's a very useful question. Knowing what our fantasies are telling us about what we want can be helpful for discovering what we are trying to work out internally. Fantasy is one way to examine our inner life to find out more about what we want or need or feel we lack in our lives. In this way, interpreting fantasy is the same as interpreting a dream. Fantasies are waking dreams. In dreams we find our wishes and our fears.

Clues to Our Truth

When we say that someone is "living in a fantasy world," it's not a compliment. We're saying, in effect, that that person is using fantasy to cut himself or herself off from others and from reality. Fantasies can either prompt us to withdraw into our own world or provide vivid images of our inner longings. Once we become conscious of the role our fantasies play in our internal life, they give us different perspectives about ourselves and what we want from loved ones. With this information we can communicate our fantasy life to our partner, which provides a glimpse into our inner world and helps us become more intimate. So destroying myth and fantasy is not the aim. Allowing them to teach us about our internal life and then expressing them provides us with valuable clues about our internal life and the reality of what's truly important to us.

Let's look at the fantasy connected with seeing someone at a party or walking down the street and deciding that this is our perfect partner, the one who will make us happy for the rest of our lives. What this fantasy may also be revealing is what's missing from our life. Perhaps we feel lonely, emotionally dead, or unlovable. The person we're looking at suddenly makes us feel more alive and excited. Fantasy, then, is creating a better feeling about ourselves and our seemingly empty life. It may also bring to light our fears, such as the fear of being truly close to someone. It may expose a sense of loss or personal numbness. For example, our fantasy about a chance meeting on an airplane and finding our true love may really be about our need to feel wanted. Or our fantasy of power and domination may really be about our own feeling of being powerless. And this in turn may reveal possibilities for making our life work better.

I'm reminded of a patient who was very involved in sadomasochistic rituals. For a while his girlfriend went along with his desire to have her submissive at all times, but soon after they were married she no longer wanted to comply with his every wish. This enraged him and he withdrew in silence. But after talking at length about his fantasies of domination, he discovered that they contained a complex set of processes that went way back to his childhood. What came up was this: his domination fantasies were more about his feelings of weakness and powerlessness than they were about his need to have his wife accept total submission. He discovered that these fantasies had come into being during adolescence and were related to his controlling and dominating mother. Once he realized where they were coming from, he was able to release his all-or-nothing stance. He and his wife worked out a way to play out some of his fantasies during sex, as a way to connect, but otherwise live a more equal life together.

This is how fantasy can help us to learn about reality and what we really need and want. Our fantasies are often vivid reflections of our internal strivings—what we deeply long for, what our truth is. Our personal myths can illuminate our fallibility, our foibles, and our sense of being somehow fraudulent or flawed. When we listen to what they tell us, we can learn from our wishes and our wounds to grasp what is most meaningful.

THE IDEAL AND THE REAL

For all the valuable information they contain, deeply held myths may also create expectations that can damage or detract from our connection with our partner. For example, if we expect love to make us happy, we are pushing away our entire past and present. Ultimately, we can't use myth to whitewash our pain; if we try to do that we will only be disappointed. Myths can distort reality, especially the popular myth of unconditional love. In the beginning of a new relationship, loving feelings appear intense and fully formed with little or no effort. It is only over months and years that the full complexity of loving another person becomes known. After years of living with another person, love is truly something that we must actively create. The myth of unconditional love without intimacy-work will ultimately set up idealistic expectations sure to cause conflicts that may break our emotional connection with our partner.

The collision between myth and reality can occur in what appear to be commonly held beliefs. The Hollywood-Western cowboy myth, for example—the ideal of the strong male character who knows what he wants and spares nothing to get it, or the strong, silent, walk-alone type—are commonly held cultural myths about love and manhood. But to find what's true about relationships we must look past the prevailing myths. We must search for what it means to be who we are in our own humanity. To understand myth and fantasy, we need to grasp what is essential about being human. In this sense we need to know what is at the core of our relationships with others. John Bowlby, the father of modern attachment theory, once said, "There is no such thing as self-sufficiency, only effective or ineffective dependency." What he meant was, like it or not, we need one another. We suffer when we live life alone; we thrive when we feel loved. Bowlby believed that at the heart of what it means to be human is the need for social contact with others. Happiness can be seen as a balance between creating our own happiness and doing things with others that make us happy. Part of that is the love and support we give to and receive from our mate.

"Matchmaker, Matchmaker, Make Me a Match"

Internet dating has created a whole new screen to project our fantasies, myths, and ideals on. We can log on at any time and see the profiles of prospective mates—not the real people, but their idealized idea of themselves. People put their best foot forward, describing their most acceptable traits and their own fantasies about romance. But there is frequently an immense difference between the presentation on a website and the person who shows up at the coffee shop. People creating profiles don't usually include poor self-esteem, hatred of their mothers or fathers, abandonment issues, fears of intimacy, or addictions in their list of personal characteristics.

Although the Internet has provided a much-needed "cyber town hall," connections that start there can be risky. Importantly, no matter what we read in a profile, the reality of this person is undoubtedly much more complex. It takes time to flush out the real person from the mythology. For this reason, when considering a new relationship with someone you've met online—or with anyone, for that matter—it's a good idea to work in some questions. *Have you ever taken time to get to know yourself? What was it like growing up? What was your relationship with your parents like? How did your mother and father treat each other? Did they express love toward one another? Did you spend a lot of time alone as a child? Did drugs, alcohol, or violence play a role in your family?* These are not easy questions, because they may tell us a lot about what is going on inside. If we encounter some startling answers to these questions, it doesn't necessarily mean we should run for the hills. It should make us want to find out more, let some time go by, and see how this person reacts to new experiences before we make up our mind. Ben Franklin once said, "Choose your bed and your shoes wisely because you will be in one or the other all your life." I would add a committed relationship to that list.

Family Myths

Families customarily mythologize themselves as happy, caring, and supportive, but behind that bright appearance there may be a darker reality that is not openly expressed. The old-fashioned notion that families should never air their "dirty laundry" in public may mean that their dark interior is hidden from everyone, often leaving bad behavior unchecked. These dark family secrets may include depression, drug addiction, alcoholism, violence, sexual abuse, or neglect. And they may follow us into our own relationships unless we separate ourselves from our family's secret myths.

Becoming our own person is not so easy, but it may be critical to making an emotional separation from what didn't work in our family of origin. The process of separation-individuation is a critical step in the process of developing a mature and healthy relationship. Robert Kegan discusses the process in his book *In Over Our Heads,* talking about maturity as a set of stages—from the first to the fourth order, or the fully actualized self—and painting a nuanced picture of the new relationship (as opposed to a clean break) that we forge with what he terms the "family religion":

The idea that leaving the third order of consciousness is akin to leaving the family religion does not mean that the move to modernity of necessity requires us to leave the family or the religion. What it requires is that we construct a new relationship to the family or the religion. Like all such metaphors sent in to aid the remaking of mind, the new spaces it can create are not necessarily separations between people but distinctions within a person, differentiations within a relationship or a faith. The prospect of leaving the family religion can foster a host of such distinctions: the distinction between having a religion and being had by one's religion; between believing as my parents believed and believing as I believe because it's how my parents believed and believing some of what my parents believed because I have come to find it is also what I believe; between finding my own way of practicing what is still a form of the family religion and leaving the faith altogether; between leaving behind some of what my parents believed and leaving behind my precious sense of connection to them. The creation of such distinctions builds a trembling bridge from the third to the fourth order of consciousness.

For most of us, the road to our separate identity can be confusing because it's so hard to know where our family leaves off and we begin. Our values and our identity, including our own brand of mythology, are the result of our entire life experience, which includes family, friendships, community, religion, and cultural education. Even though some of what we believed as children has proven not to be true, we switch back in time automatically as the impression of a previous experience is stimulated in the present. Part of knowing ourselves better is to understand what has affected us. Our experience belongs to us; it makes up a large part of who we are. To push away or deny parts of ourselves creates separations within us. Learning to look at ourselves objectively and accept how our history has affected us not only creates internal clarity but also helps prevent us from becoming fragmented victims of our past.

When couples can draw distinctions between their individual form of a "family religion" and what they have come to believe as a couple, they are building a "trembling bridge" between their two worlds. A lasting intimacy is created by the blending of mutually formed values and shaped by an agreed-upon sense of what is satisfying to each. To distinguish how their personal, romantic, and family myths play out between them offers hope for a new beginning and the possibility of a more profound loving experience.

Myth and Marriage

We live in a culture of romantic concoctions, potions, and palliatives with equally high sets of expectations. For couples contemplating marriage, romantic expectations can sometimes overburden the relationship altogether. Ted Huston, PhD, a professor of psychology at the University of Texas, carried out a long-term study on newly married couples. He called it the PAIR project, an acronym for Processes of Adaptation in Intimate Relationships, and followed 168 couples through the first two years of marriage. He found that couples who began their relationships with a high degree of romantic mythology and high expectations about what love should be had a more difficult time adjusting to married life than those who started out with more realistic expectations of marriage. An old saying claims that there is an inverse ratio between the size of the wedding and the length of the marriage, because large weddings are so romantically charged that the mundanity of modern marriage can be a huge letdown. According to Huston, couples who held to a highly unrealistic romantic mythology were more likely to become disenchanted. Couples who did not try to maintain the romantic ideal were less conflicted. Of those in the study who got divorced, most stated that it was the loss of their original romantic feelings that originally caused their alienation from one another. To these couples, the natural ebb and flow of emotions was a signal that their romantic myth had failed them. They were quick to conclude that there was something fundamentally wrong with the marriage when they lost the original "spark" of romantic love.

Huston contends that marriage is nourished more by supporting positive feelings than by spending time trying to fix what's wrong, especially when what's wrong may be impossible to change, like a high-strung personality or a tendency to be messy or compulsively fastidious. Couples who are desperately trying to maintain their original romantic mythology will be sorely disappointed when conflicts that are a natural part of living cannot be resolved. But couples who understand that ambivalent states of love and anger can coexist in normal love relationships are more likely to stay together. Huston suggests that whirlwind romances bode poorly for marital success because they paint an unrealistic picture of a future that often cannot be realized. In contrast, Huston offers an "enduring dynamics" model in which stability and predictability determine marital success more often than constant happiness and romance.

In the novel *Corelli's Mandolin*, by Louis de Bernières, the wise Dr. Iannis describes his view of mature love to his daughter, speaking to what it means to feel deeply for another person with whom one has lived for many years:

Love is a temporary madness. It erupts like an earthquake and then subsides. And when it subsides you have to make a decision. You have to work out whether your roots have become so entwined together that it is inconceivable that you should ever part. Because this is what love is. Love is not breathlessness, it is not excitement and it is not the promulgation of promises of eternal passion. That is just being in love, which any of us can convince ourselves we are.

Love itself is what is left over when being in love has burned away, and this is both an art and a fortunate accident. Your mother and I had it, we had roots that grew towards each other underground, and when all the pretty blossoms had fallen from our branches, we found that we were one tree and not two.

THE MYTH OF REDEMPTION

Redemption is an act of forgiveness, even absolution, for behaviors or thoughts past and present that we have never made peace with. It registers as a relief from feelings of loss, shame, or guilt that have been eradicated through a redemptive act. Our hope for redemption may be based on a fantasy that contains a myth, such as the myth that love heals all and the fantasy that this certain person will cure our feelings of inadequacy. Or it may be about reclaiming something that was lost: if we were abused as children, then humiliating someone in retaliation may be a form of redemption. Someone who felt unwanted as a child may attempt to be desired by as many others as possible. A man may obsessively work to be wealthy so he can be redeemed from feeling valueless. A woman who grew up poor and felt ashamed of her poverty may believe in the myth that marrying a rich man will redeem her.

The fantasy that someone will make us whole, adequate, and lovable is not uncommon. Romantic myths tell us that love will redeem us from loneliness. Redemptive fantasies of perfection, financial success, or being desired are all attempts at changing something bad into something good. The myth that someone can save us from ourselves is a powerful source of hope—but ultimately, seeking love as redemption for our personal misery never works, precisely because it's based on a myth. Falling in love can offer only temporary relief from inner misery. Realistically, our partner cannot always be available and will not be able to always meet our needs.

The difficulty with redemptive myths and fantasies is that they alter reality. Understanding the reality of what relationships *can* provide allows us to look into the truth about what we really want. To do this, it's important to understand that redemptive fantasies can be traced back to our earliest experiences. They originate from our coping strategies for getting along with our family. Many children grow into adulthood never realizing that they felt alone; they may have mistaken duty or admiration for love, while inwardly hurting and not knowing why. Our effort to find Mr. or Ms. Right is often a fantasy-fueled quest to heal our deep sense of loneliness and redeem us from our sense of worthlessness. Once we've found our ideal person and gotten married, though, the lonely feelings that have lain dormant for years may break open, and along with them depression, anxiety, and angry defensiveness. If our mate fails to measure up to some aspect of our early coping happily-ever-after mythology, it may stimulate the old sad and angry feelings all over again. Then we turn on our mate and blame him or her for our unhappiness, creating conflict that makes us unhappier still. This is how a redemptive fantasy can turn counterproductive.

Broken Arrow

When Helen and Jim first came in for couple therapy, she was hopeless and he was worn out. It was immediately clear that this young couple did not understand what was causing their arguments and could not identify what was wrong between them. Helen had thought she was marrying her ideal man, and consequently she was deeply disappointed in what turned out to be her real husband. Jim, for his part, thought when he married Helen that she was totally accepting of him, so he was completely surprised to find that she was critical and unhappy with him. They had lost hope that their difficulties could be resolved.

Helen described a painful childhood. She was physically abused by her father, and her mother's alcoholism and subsequent depression prevented her from coming to her daughter's aid. In fact, her mother's fragile emotional states turned Helen into a caretaker herself. She became a mother substitute to her sisters. To distract herself from her misery, she dreamed that someday her prince would come to save her from her loneliness and feelings of being unlovable. The redemptive fantasy had these two missions and neither would be accomplished. The loss of redemption left her devastated, hopeless, and angry.

When Helen met Jim, he seemed to be the savior she had always dreamed of. She was 35 years old and felt that if she didn't grab this guy fast she might not get another chance at having a family. She pushed hard to become exactly what Jim wanted her to be so they could speed along toward marriage.

Jim's parents were college professors who placed a tremendous value on education and scholarly performance. Although Jim had been able to achieve academically, he felt his parents paid almost no attention to who he was inside. He feared that the approval he got from them was based solely on his ability to perform in school. Jim's mother was a perfectionist and withdrew when he made mistakes. As Jim matured, he dreamed of marrying a woman who would love him for who he really was. He wanted to be accepted for himself, not because of what he could achieve.

During their courtship, Helen and Jim lived in different cities and commuted to see each other on the weekends. The distance allowed them to create romantic fantasies about each other and their relationship that in effect shielded them from seeing any deeper issues. When they got together on the weekends, they were active socially and spent little time alone. They didn't often speak of their inner life or how they had suffered, because they were largely unaware of the effects of their early experience. When they were first married, they continued to be gregarious, traveling with friends and engaging in social activities.

Soon into their marriage, they decided to have a child. As Jim became more successful as a stockbroker, they decided Helen should stay home and raise their daughter, but soon difficulties began to arise. Helen wanted Jim to be handy around the house, but he procrastinated because he was insecure and scared that she would be critical of him. Helen's perfectionism reminded him of his mother and made him feel inadequate, so he shut down. He would experience anxiety attacks when asked to do something as simple as changing a light bulb. Helen, in turn, saw his difficulty with household work as proof that he didn't love her. She would upbraid him for his passivity or explode with rage at what she considered his laziness. (Even during our sessions, she sat as far away from him as she could except to blurt out angry phrases like "He's a slug.") This would cause Jim to become sullen or act superior, responding with "I have better things to do than change light bulbs—that's your job." Jim and Helen were powerless to resolve their conflicts because they didn't know how to express their real complaints.

Helen wanted Jim to be her ideal man. Her knight would rise early and shoulder part of the childcare load by getting their daughter ready for school. Then he would be off to work with a spring in his step. Her ideal man would listen, complete projects on his own, and be an overall ultra-responsible, sensitive, caring, and proactive New Age kind of guy. Based on this idealized version of a husband, Helen was despondent about what seemed to her a horrible choice.

Jim, though he was a procrastinator and not attentive in the ways Helen wished, was otherwise a loving husband and father. *His* fantasy was that Helen would provide the emotional acceptance he had never felt from his mother. He believed during their courtship that she was the perfect woman. As she became critical, he responded by withdrawing as his mother had done to him, but this only infuriated Helen. He had tried everything but could not make her happy. He felt woefully inadequate, and Helen's criticism of him only confirmed his worst fears about himself. When Jim did not do what Helen expected of him, she would take it personally—"If he really loved me, he would help me and keep his promises"—and when he tried to defend himself, she would lash out at him. He bitterly and righteously complained, "I'm damned if I do, and I'm damned if I don't."

As their sessions became more and more heated, I decided to see them individually for several sessions to de-escalate the anger and find out more about what was at the bottom of their conflicts. This required some psychotherapy to determine where their wounds were and to make them aware of how the wounds affected their relationship. Interestingly, both Helen and Jim were different in their private sessions than in their couple sessions. One-on-one with me, they were able to see what was going on psychologically in a way that they couldn't do when they were together. This gave me an idea about how to treat the problem. I could tell that they had the ability to be sensitive and flexible with me; I felt that if they could translate that same process into their relationship, then we might just be able to work toward resolution. And indeed, as Helen and Jim started to feel even more comfortable in their intimacy with me, with some urging they began to open up to each other too. What we discovered was that neither of them had fully internalized a commitment to their marriage. They believed deep down that divorce was a way out. They were always secretly preparing to leave. When they finally decided they wanted to make a full commitment to their marriage, they could accept that it was up to them to make it better.

The expectations of redemptive fantasy were the culprits here. Helen and Jim tried to live their fantasy ideal and it just didn't fit with reality. Instead, it operated as a mask to hide their fear and loneliness. Helen's romantic fantasies were a means of defending against her fear of abandonment. They offered her a sense of possibility and hope. When she couldn't be perfect, it opened the door to her internalized anger, causing her to be righteous and vengeful. This made Jim feel inadequate and he retaliated by passive withdrawal, which angered Helen no end. *When they finally opened up, out came two angry children who were terrified to be seen for who they thought they really were.*

We decided to do some more individual therapy to work on self-esteem issues and anger and build skills they could use to express their wishes, desires, and needs. Because they had been so emotionally withdrawn, as they learned to communicate their needs, fears, and concerns, their relationship improved and the anger subsided. They learned to communicate with each other in a way that helped each of them meet their individual needs, and this affected their mood and sense of hope about the future. It was clear that for this couple, individual psychological issues were affecting the way they related to each other. Their mythic expectations were emanating from infantile longings, unmet needs, and painful experiences. As we cleared up the personal issues and resumed their couple sessions, the relationship calmed down. As of this writing, Helen and Jim are still together and have had another child. They learned that if one of them is having a problem, it doesn't mean there is a loss of love.

One Piece of the Puzzle

The example of Helen and Jim teaches us something about commitment. Helen held on to the option of leaving so she wouldn't have to come face-to-face with her pain and low self-esteem. Instead of prompting her to work through her personal and relationship problems, her mythology served to strengthen her resolve that Jim was not the right man for her. Mythology in this instance operated as a defense against looking at painful personal issues. When couples make deep commitments, then the work is to go after issues, not run away from them through romantic fantasy. To deepen her commitment to her relationship, Helen had to look beyond her mythology to her emotional problems. Her dedication to the marriage hardened her resolve to face her personal demons and understand how they affected her relationship with Jim.

Statistics show that unmarried couples who live together have a much lower success rate than married couples, who are by definition committed to staying together. The deeper the commitment, the harder people work. They have a stake in making their relationship run more smoothly. When Helen and Jim finally made a commitment to making their marriage work, instead of looking for the exit door—and using myths and fantasies to do it—they worked to find solutions because it was in both of their best interests.

The idea of commitment, however, is not an end in itself. Commitment involves the day-to-day activity of making love work. It does not mean that simply being committed is the answer, because there are no pat answers. If we decide to be honest, with an open mind, we will have a better chance at a lasting relationship. If we believe that there is something better just over the horizon, it will weaken our commitment.

Gertrude Stein is famous for saying, "There is no there there." In relationships, there is no there to get to; it's right in front of us. The grass turns out not to be greener on the other side. And as Buckaroo Banzai once said, "No matter where you go, there you are." Our issues will follow us everywhere we go, and to think that some one thing will save us from ourselves is unrealistic. Relationship happiness is an active process and requires external support and internal acceptance. Learning about our personal mythology, our fantasy life, and how it affects the way we see the reality of relationships is an important step to finding love in the real world. Loving each other, finding interesting work, developing our personal life, and finding the joy in gratitude and forgiveness are the other essentials of happiness. So it may not be in our nature to always be happy, but it is the pursuit of happiness that can help to define what it means to us. Happiness really happens from the inside out, and myths and fantasy provide a true glimpse into the interior of our soul. To see and understand the logic of our myths and fantasies offers up not only our own wishes and truth, but the path to a better life and a more loving future.

MOONLIGHT AND THE LIGHT OF DAY

Helen and Jim's story gives us a vivid example of how romantic ideals and mythology, both personal and interpersonal, can come between couples and stand in the way of true loving connections. These processes work entirely on their own until we shine a light on them and see how and why they operate as they do. Only then can we change the way they influence our behavior and our ability to relate to others. Now let's take a closer look at how and why we build up these ideals and, conversely, how we can swing so far in the other direction that we tear our partners down.

Idealization

Stephen Mitchell, acclaimed author, poet, and translator, writes, "What makes someone desirable is idealization, an act of imagination that highlights the qualities that make that person unique, special, out of the ordinary." To create an object of desire in this way requires a leap beyond the ordinary—and something real is lost in the process: Mitchell goes on to call idealizations "the product of artificial sweeteners." When idealizations fail, as they always do, we are left with reality. So, idealizations set us up for a fall. In this way idealizations are akin to fantasy. When we first meet someone, we are immersed in a romantic idealized fantasy. In the moonlight everything appears to be perfect. But idealization inevitably gives way to disappointment as the relationship progresses and we start to see the object of desire in the cold light of day. Eventually that disappointment, if not addressed and worked through, may lead to devaluation, disillusionment, and alienation.

The theory behind idealization goes like this: all infants and children idealize their parents; they must do this to stay attached and neutralize their fear of abandonment. Idealization is a part of healthy maturation. For example, superheroes and children's dolls are idealized/mythic figures and models for adult behavior. Heroes and dolls embody values and images of strength that children use to help them ward off fears, define healthy identities, and move toward becoming fully formed adults. Idealization can also be a kind of saving grace for one's inner fears of abandonment and helplessness—and the more unavailable the parent is, the greater the need for fantasy to ease the fears. Idealization is a fantasy itself, but a different sort: it is a fantasy about the other, more based in reality than in pure fantasy that has less to do with the real world. In brief, a child idealizes his mother to make her better than she is so he can stay more securely attached. He may fantasize an image of her when she is absent for the same reason.

For children to psychologically survive their rage at the mother and the fear of abandonment, rage must be "split off" from consciousness because expressing these feelings may drive her further away. If the mother is unavailable for too long, the anger created from the pain of loneliness and fear of abandonment is withdrawn because to feel it or express it would be too painful. (This same anger that is pulled inside for safety will be expressed toward lovers in adulthood.) As experiences of rejection add up, the child may try to be perfect as a means of enticing the mother to come closer and accept him. In this way the idealized fantasy and the defenses work together.

Devaluation: The Other Side of the Coin

When the child matures into adulthood and brings his idealization with him, a host of troubles can arise from his fantasy-based view of how relationships should be. It's then that devaluation can rear its ugly head. Idealization based on the fear of abandonment develops into devaluation on the same basis, to protect us from being hurt. Devaluation is essentially a defense against rejection and dependence: if children are rejected repeatedly when they seek affection or connection with their parents, they come to believe that their needs are bad and that to depend on anyone only leads to rejection. The more we devalue people, the less we have to need them. We have rendered them worthless. This process is entirely unconscious, so many people with this problem find the same situation coming up in every relationship. No one is good enough; everyone starts out idealized, then falls from grace and is tossed on the slagheap with the many who have come before.

Here are some common ways that devaluation can work:

- **Hitting below the belt**: Once you devalue your partner enough, you feel entitled to hit below the belt, using your knowledge of his soft spots to hurt him and to push him away. In this way devaluation allows for retaliation and disconnection, the ultimate move to safety.

- **Injustice collecting**: Collecting devaluations is another method of creating distance and safety. After you have internally and secretly devalued your mate for a long period of time, you can let her have it all at once, in one giant explosion. Then you can feel righteous, satisfied that you are right and good and she's bad and wrong.

- **Displacement**: Another way to devalue your partner is to make him responsible for your bad day. When the traffic was horrible, or your boss blamed you for someone else's mistake, or your mother made you feel guilty, these feelings can easily be projected onto your mate. You lash out or become depressed about experiences that have nothing to do with him, and yet you somehow feel he is responsible for them.

- **Intellectualization:** This defense is all head and no heart. It's analytical and protects us against being hurt because we've walled off our emotional world so no one can touch it. Intellectualization is safe. We don't have to engage our feelings. If we are analyzing, we are not sympathizing or engaging our partner emotionally. For this reason, intellectualization is one of the best defenses against the fear of being hurt or being intimate.

For the vast majority of people this activity is entirely unconscious and often automatic. But couples can learn to bypass the trap and instead express their deeply felt needs for love and affection. They can learn to detect when the signs of idealization and devaluation appear, and they can neutralize the effect by defining what they need and want from each other in the moment. In this way they can respond to their internal promptings and create connection. Idealization and devaluation are defenses against feelings and needs. If we can neutralize our shame about having needs and allow ourselves to depend on our mate for love and affection, we will have a mutually satisfying relationship. If we can bring reality into our idealizations about our romantic fantasies, we may prevent that terrible fall from the pedestal.

FROM MYTH TO REALITY

Many years ago I heard writer and Harvard psychologist Carol Gilligan speak at a conference entitled "Passionate Attachments." In her speech, as in her groundbreaking book *In a Different Voice,* she said, "Love is what happens when the cracks in our ideals heal up." She made the very important point that we all idealize, but we also have to know that the idealized image will shatter into pieces at some point and that putting those pieces back together is what love is all about. If we put the pieces back with care, insight, empathy, and love, we will build something stronger than the original. If we don't, our relationship may end up just a mass of broken glass.

In every relationship, we experience disruptions in our ideal of love that lead inevitably to disappointment. Love is the result of healing those breaks in our ideal (our myth) of what a relationship should be. We may begin by believing in the idealized myth of perfect love, but in time we come to the realization that we're living with a human being who has foibles and flaws. If we understand the difference between idealized myth and reality, we will naturally become more compassionate toward our loved ones. Reconciling the difference between fantasy, idealizations, myths, and reality is the work of creating love.

Love that endures is not sustained by chemistry alone, but fashioned from the desire to be with that one person, in reality, in truth. Expecting our myths to come true can only create conflict and break connections. When romantic myths fail us, we are left with a sense of loss, and we may feel the urge to find someone new to fit into our mythology. If we go that route, we will only be disappointed all over again.

Reality Check

Understanding the relationship between fantasy, myth, and realistic expectations is crucial to relationship happiness and mature love. But with romantic misinformation being hurled at us from all sides, how can we avoid the lure of myth and fantasy? We need a clear sense of reality—the true building block for lasting love. The challenge is to know how to find it. The question we must ask ourselves is: how invested are we in the idea of love as a salvation or a cure for what ails us? Knowing how our attitudes are shaped by culture and experience helps us to see more clearly into who we are and what we are about. If we grasp what we really want out of our lives, what makes us happy, what our values are, and how they fit into the way we are with our partner, we won't be disappointed when our love relationship has its own set of difficulties. We will know what we need to do because we have done our own research into what we want and where we are headed.

The search for what is real is an active, ongoing process of thought and dialogue with others we trust. A set of realistic expectations for love can give us a place to start.

Realistic Expectations

- Our feelings ebb and flow.

- Relationships require perseverance.

- Ambivalence is expected.

- Conflict is inevitable.

- Differences are desirable.

- Trust is earned.

- Kindness is crucial.

- Empathy is required.

- Humor helps.

- Sometimes saying nothing works best.

- We can't change our mates.

- Acceptance creates peace.

Getting There from Here

Understanding how our feelings change from our romantic beginnings requires that we know something about what causes those changes to occur. In the normal course of events, feelings toward our mate flow in and out organically, riding the constantly shifting tides of emotion. Most people experience a full range of emotions and moods, from love to annoyance, from comfort to anger, from commitment to ambivalence, from joy to displeasure, from passion to jealousy. When couples accept that romantic feelings continually ebb and flow, they become more firmly planted in reality.

Relationships that last do so because the people in them understand how to make grief important, pain productive, and conflict a learning experience. We'll examine all these processes more closely in the chapters ahead. Intimacy is made out of good communication, the acceptance of differences, perseverance, the capacity for tenderness, the ability to bear ambivalence, and the desire for peaceful problem-solving. When couples can make space for pathos, turmoil, and confusion and still maintain their sense of balance, they will survive, even prosper, in the changing landscape of intimacy.

For Your Inter-Reflection

Myth, Fantasy, and Reality

1. What myths did you come into your relationship with? How have they changed over time?

2. Would you say you are not getting what you want from your relationship? Why not? What do you think would make it better?

3. Make a list of the things you feel your relationship should be giving you, then make a list of the things you are getting. Note the items on the first list that aren't on the second. Which are based on idealizations and which are based in reality?

4. After reading this chapter, has your concept of realistic expectations for your relationship changed? If so, how?

5. Write down a list of fantasies for your relationship. Ask your partner to do the same, if he or she is willing. Share your lists.

shame, rage, and myths of the self

*We live in an atmosphere of shame. We are ashamed of
everything that is real about us; ashamed of ourselves, of our
relatives, of our incomes, of our accents, of our opinions, of
our experience, just as we are ashamed of our naked skins.*

—George Bernard Shaw

FALLING IN LOVE IS A POTENT FORCE that stimulates our deepest
longings, wishes, hopes, and dreams, but also the pain and suffering of our past. In the last chapter, we saw the influence that myths
about ourselves can exert on our lives; personal myths that are
formed from unprocessed painful experiences are especially powerful, as they can lead us into self-criticism, self-blaming, and self-
destructive behavior that may ultimately damage our relationships
as well.

The psychological term that best describes the effect of painful
life experiences is the word *shame*. Shame wounds sustained in
childhood can influence our behavior in a variety of ways. Shame is
complex, as are the patterns of relating into which it leads us and the
defenses it builds to protect us from further harm. In this chapter,

we'll look at how shame arises, how it can manifest as rage in our intimate relationships, and how we can overcome its obstacles.

BAD SELF, BAD OTHER

The word *shame* comes to us from the Germanic word *skamo*, which in turn owes its origins to the Proto-Indo-European root word *skem-*, derived from *kem-*, meaning to cover or to hide. The Talmud warns that "shaming another in public is like shedding blood." Whether we fantasize that someone is shaming us or whether the injury is real, shame is the root cause of many conflicts in relationships.

Shame is our personal reaction to acts of humiliation, rejection, abandonment, or neglect. It is a sinking feeling of being cast out or perhaps even openly humiliated. Feelings of shame relate to our belief that we are essentially worthless, weak, inadequate, or bad—a deeply held belief that is often unknown even to us. Psychologist Silvan Tomkins identified neural pathways in the brain that are specifically targeted to shame, discovering, in essence, that shame reactions are hard-wired into our system. (Interestingly, Tomkins also found that shame and joy are connected to the same neural pathway in the brain. This may mean that we are especially shame-prone when we're happy.) These feelings can be generated at any time in life but are especially powerful when experienced in childhood. Shame wounds eventually form into our personal identity; they are essentially about who we are.

Shame is not the same as guilt, though they often occur together. Guilt is typically associated with our reaction to breaks in our moral or ethical behavior. We can feel as guilty about our thoughts as we can about our actions. We may feel guilty about not doing things that we think we "should" be doing. We may feel guilty about our dishonesty, our greed, our selfishness, or being mean to someone we love. It's felt as a tearing away from our moral ideal for good behavior. Shame and guilt can be experienced at the same time: "I did something bad (guilt) and I did it because I'm bad (shame)."

We may compensate for our shameful sense of self by behaving in ways that are the opposite of how we really feel. For example, we may compensate for feeling shy and undeserving by trying to be perfect. We may act out angrily in response to the small slights of everyday life. And the shame we feel about ourselves may explode in the form of rage at something or someone outside us. Rage emanating from shame is essentially a paranoid process because it originates within us and is directed toward the other, even before we are conscious of the feeling. Paranoid ideation means that bad feelings about ourselves are propelled outward, psychologically thrown out of our system to reappear as dangerous or negative images outside us. In this way rage bypasses the "bad self" and projects it out, forming "bad other."

When children who have suffered shaming events mature and develop relationships of their own, their pent-up rage is turned against others during stressful times. A man arrives home from a hellish day at work. His wife immediately hands him their baby, saying, "You take her. I'm so exhausted I can't see straight." If the man's early experiences have left him prone to shame—and especially if something made him feel humiliated earlier in the day—he may become enraged at his wife's request: "Do you think I'm your slave? I work my ass off all day, and you have no appreciation for what I do. Instead you want me to take over your job as soon as I walk in the door. You're pathetic." The transformation from a perceived humiliation to shame and then to rage is swift and destructive. His response will cause a break in their emotional connection, and continued responses like this, especially if accompanied by any form of violence, may eventually end their relationship.

Neutralizing the toxic effect of shame requires that we learn how to stop self-criticism and self-blame, view our past with compassion, and allow ourselves to grieve over the losses and pain that created our shame reaction. Taking time to consider our needs and feelings will help us to take better care of ourselves and stay healthy—one of the best ways of neutralizing shame. The paradox is that shame makes us do the opposite of what is healthy. So we must heal first and then by small steps begin a healthy life.

THE ROOTS OF SHAME AND RAGE

Shame wounds originate deep in our past. At their most basic, they are caused by a failure of empathy from parents, caregivers, or loved ones. Empathy, quite simply, is the ability to gain insight into the experience of the other person. Infants and children are themselves unable to empathize with their caregivers and therefore can't understand what is hurting them. They don't have the ability to think abstractly that they are being hurt; they only know that they are hurting. They are not able to understand that someone else may be humiliating them, nor can they recognize what is causing it. They experience everything as "me"—including a shaming event. For children, shaming is especially frightening and unbearable, because they transform these bad experiences into a bad self.

Ten thousand years ago, if a child was left alone for more than a few minutes, he became lunch for a wild animal. Our brain still functions as if we are living 10,000 years ago. We react to isolation, rejection, or abandonment as if it were life-threatening. So children respond to neglect as if their lives are literally in jeopardy, and the psyche closes ranks to protect them. Their survival instincts kick in, and since they can't retaliate toward a rejecting parent for fear they will be pushed even further away, they turn on themselves instead.

Out of terror and desperation to maintain the connection to the parent, the child must idealize the parent and devalue the self. This self-blaming creates a self-critical stance, an antagonistic relationship within the self that can last a lifetime. (The parent is often an active participant in this interchange, because he or she may also blame the child for the problem.) The pain and rage brought on by rejection and humiliation must be effectively concealed in order to preserve the fragile bond with the parent or caretaker. The brain, which is in charge of protecting the child from harm, steals away pain for safekeeping, and shame along with it. These intense and severe shame experiences will eventually exert influence over the child's behavior, but from a separate place within the self, where defenses are formed as protection from further isolation, abandonment, or humiliation.

About Attachment

Noted psychiatrist Dr. M. J. Barry describes the early shame experience this way:

> Shame originates from the parent's attitude toward the child, being an angry rejection of the child himself. The parent attacks the child's right to their behavior and degrades the child. This is usually followed by an angry rejection of the child. The child through similar onslaughts is forced into the humiliating feeling that they are worth less than the parent is worth. They fear abandonment, they fear their own anger and resentment, and they suffer the loss of confidence in their own reactions or the ability to control their rage. The distance that the parent creates from their rejection of the child because of his/her badness leaves the child alone in painful solitude.

The shame scene Dr. Barry is describing may be set off by a temper tantrum that is quite normal for that developmental stage, just a phase the child is going through. A child may not know how to ask for affection, and because the parent has not provided a way for him to express his needs, he will fall into a tantrum as a last-ditch effort to get the attention he craves. His parents may decide to correct this "bad" behavior by rejecting or punishing him. The child may feel humiliated, and he may connect this shameful experience to his needs for affection and attention. In adulthood he will have a very difficult time expressing his needs for affection and attention, and he will rage at his partner for not knowing how to meet the needs he can't express.

Earlier in this book, we talked about attachment theory—an area of great interest in psychology today that deals with defining the quality of the emotional connections we form early in life and the consequences for our later relationships. Shame and rage are founded on particularly poor attachment with the parent. Neglect and abuse create intense rage states that sever attachments when we are children and continue to do so when we are adults. In these rage states, there is a primitive desire to attach, a deep sense of longing for the other person to feel what we feel, and in this way it is a search for intimacy, even a primitive attempt at empathy. All behavior has meaning. We need to understand what problem our behavior is trying to solve. What are we doing to try to get our needs met or work through our pain?

Should We Blame the Parents?

The problem of blaming the parents remains a very difficult one for psychotherapists and patients because our need to be loyal to our parents naturally leads us to lay the responsibility for our problems on some essential flaw within us. But the fact is that though parents try to do their best, they may not provide the necessary emotional connections, support, or nurturing we need and as a result may unintentionally harm us. Most parents are doing what they know and what they learned from their own parents, who might have been very limited in their emotional resources and even abusive. When we can understand that a series of negative experiences is what has created our negative self-image, we can eventually build a true sense of who we are. Not that we must reject or even confront our parents, but in accepting them as human beings we humanize them and ourselves.

To develop emotional health we need to understand that self-blaming and the shame it causes can be toxic to us and to our relationships. The key point in looking at the role our caretakers played in our identity formation, or the lack of it, is not to blame them or use them to excuse our behavior, but simply to see clearly how they affected us. Understanding our history not only helps us alleviate self-blame, criticism, depression, anxiety, and violence, but also provides important insights into the workings of our present intimate relationships.

Whatever we do not understand about ourselves and our past will be transported into our present. If we deny our essential wounds, they will surface without our knowledge and drive a wedge into our relationships with others. Our understanding of what has shaped us allows us to make contact with the love that lies just beneath. Understanding what we feel, want, and need makes it more possible to be intimate with our mate. This awareness allows us to distinguish between ourselves and our mate so when disputes do arise we can understand what our contribution to the problem actually is.

Cause and Effect

When psychologists ponder the psyche, they are most interested in studying the causes of psychological conflicts and what promotes healing. Their main focus is on what it means to be healthy, and specifically what may be preventing people from actualizing their potential or their true selves. The reason we look to family and childhood as a basis for psychological health is that children spend so much time with their parents and siblings when they are the most sensitive, dependent, and vulnerable. If we can take the negative out of blame and connect the cause with the effect, then we shift from *self-blaming* to a *cause-and-effect* reality that's based on the experiences that have made us the way we are.

Leon Wurmser writes in his classic study *The Mask of Shame* that the child is an "omnipotent masochist" because he feels responsible for causing his own pain. If his parents were cold and withholding, he experiences this as "I am inadequate and unlovable." If his parents were angry and rejecting, he believes that he is bad and useless. If his parents punished him for being angry or left him alone, he will be forced to hold in his anger and direct it at himself in a quest for perfection and redemption in his parents' eyes. If his parents were fragile and he happens to be angry, this fragility might cause him to withhold his anger or deny it altogether.

In an article in the *Journal of Counseling Psychology,* Gershen Kaufman writes, "Even though the aftermath of shame can be severe, the way to a self-affirming identity yet lies in the deeply human capacity to be fully restored, in the knowledge that one individual can restore the interpersonal bridge with another however late it may be and in the awareness that human relationships are reparable. Through such restoring of the bridge, shame is transcended." These wise lines express the central theme of what it means to be human. When we experience concern, interest, and caring, we're affected positively, and this is what restores our true nature. If it's uncaring people who inflict wounds, then we need loving people to heal them. In this process we see what love and care from others means to our lives and for our very soul.

SHAME AND RAGE IN RELATIONSHIPS

Imagine our psyche as layered much like tree rings, made up of experiences that are linked together with emotional and cognitive memories as well as needs and drives such as hunger and sexuality. Or think of these rings another way, like the grooves on a record: the psyche acts like a turntable, playing our old experiences over and over again. So the needle hits the original experiential ring of shame and the old tune starts playing in our body and mind. In a flash, our internal landscape changes, triggering an intense negative response. In one-tenth of a second—the speed of a brain wave—we are reacting either by feeling shamed or with a powerful defense like rage.

The Pressure Is On

Rage is a massive physical and psychic response to a shaming event—quite distinct from anger, which is primarily a response to hurt feelings, sadness, fear, or guilt, and which is also much milder. Contrasting anger with rage is like comparing a rainstorm to a hurricane or a wave to a tsunami. Anger can be painful and counterproductive, but rage is violent and intended to injure as payback for a real or imagined offense.

Rage is an intense emotional state that is layered with both shameful feelings and complex defenses. It builds up inside and must find some way out. At a certain point the pressure builds so high that a simple request to pass the potatoes can turn into a violent episode—it takes that little to put the needle in the groove and start up the old tune. As pain becomes too intense for the system to contain, the brain creates a sense of righteousness or entitlement to justify the rage. In its own way, rage is an attempt at communication, because one partner is saying to the other, "I'll show you"—in effect, *I'll show you what it's like to hurt the way I do.* Rage can serve as an intense connection; it may be the only way certain couples can connect. The problem is that this kind of empathy is a one-way street. Even if the intention is to let the other person know how we feel, rage ultimately breaks the connection by recreating the earlier shaming event. The early idealized relationship with the brutal parent is being reenacted in the current relationship, except the victim has now become the aggressor. The aftermath is distrust, contempt, and broken hearts.

The Mind's Defenses

For the system to operate effectively, the psyche must create massive shifts in reasoning. So rage appears to the person experiencing it as if it's solely about the other. That person has sinned and must pay. Psychologists call this need for revenge "talionic," a reference to the first rule of law enacted in Babylonia about 2000 BC when King Hammurabi called for "an eye for an eye and a tooth for a tooth." This code was known as the "judgment of righteousness." The comparison is apt: rage feels entirely justified to the person experiencing it.

This is the interesting quality about rage, as well as the thing that makes it so difficult to change—the fact that the reality distortions causing people to feel entitled to rage are so real to them. They perceive rejection or humiliation even when it doesn't actually exist. Many a perpetrator has beaten his or her significant other on an assumption that arose entirely from such a primal distortion.

Paradoxically, shame and rage are governed by a part of the brain that thinks it's helping us to survive but in reality is only creating more pain. This disconnect isn't really surprising; we are often only marginally aware of the source of our behavior or how it translates into consequences. Stuart Yudofsky, MD, writes in *Fatal Flaws,* a book about personality and character disorders:

> Although their causes and presentations are often hidden and confusing, flawed personalities and character structures create wreckage that is not at all subtle. The resulting pain and suffering

can overwhelm the lives of those with whom they are importantly associated; and the related material losses are incalculable. Examples include your fiancée being unfaithful; your husband gambling away the savings for the children's college tuition; your employee stealing money from your business; your parent being abused by an attendant in a nursing home; . . . your child attending school while high on drugs; your wife injuring herself and others while driving while intoxicated . . .

Yudofsky goes on to explain that these people truly believe they don't have a problem, so they see no reason to make changes in their behavior. As we can see, their minds have created powerful defenses to ensure that their methods for expelling pain remain intact. What Yudofsky is saying here is that we may be thinking one thing in the mind, but the body will be doing something quite different. We may not want to gamble, drink, do drugs, beat our mate, or steal from our boss, but it still happens. The origins of these behaviors often bear little relation to rational thought. What therapists try to do is to combine rational thought with our need to protect ourselves—to enlist the mind to determine what the body is telling us.

A Study in Shame Wounds

Jennie and Jack had been married ten years when they arrived for their first session. Jennie had developed a career as an advertising executive and Jack worked as a computer analyst. Jack worked from home, while Jennie drove to various projects throughout the city. She was a workaholic, frequently showing up late for planned activities, which infuriated Jack.

They had had two children within the first three years of marriage. The stress it created caused frequent violent arguments. Their fights, centered on child-rearing and money, were filled with insults and personal recriminations and were utterly exhausting. They couldn't break out of the negative cycle.

As we worked together, clues to the cause of their rage began to emerge. Jennie grew up in a household with a distant, intellectual, and perfectionist father and a rather overworked career-woman mother. It felt as if her mother had opted out of Jennie's life, while her father demanded excellence. There was nowhere to hide from his verbally abusive tirades, and her mother was nowhere to be found. To cope with her father, Jennie had to internalize her anger and become as perfect as possible to mollify him. That was her response to the shaming experience of his abuse.

When Jennie got out into the world, she discovered that she was more like her parents than she had imagined. She observed herself working too much, like her mother, and having exceedingly high expectations for herself and others, just like her father. At the same time, she was still living out the effects of her flawed connection with them. When she felt angry with her husband or others, she quietly seethed, then showed up late or forgot things, just as she had done with her father to make him angry. Never being able to live up to her father's expectations fueled her adult need to overcompensate, to be perfect; her perfectionism kept her running behind schedule because she wouldn't leave home until everything was just so. Jack felt that she ran late because she didn't care about him, so they fought. Jack would demean Jennie for what he believed was a lack of concern for her family. Jennie would sit and take it for a long time, then reach her boiling point and storm out of the house. She was using Jack's criticism as an excuse to vent the built-up pain of her early shame wounds. After serious and protracted fights, there would be a period of calm, and then the cycle would begin again.

As we looked closely at Jack's family dynamic, we found more clues. It turned out that Jack's low self-esteem and anger toward Jennie could be traced back to shame of his own, rooted in his relationship with his cold, critical, and withholding mother. She was an old-fashioned disciplinarian who abused him emotionally and physically as a child. She ran a tight ship with little room for Jack's big personality. Jack's father, a traveling salesman, was often on the road; when he was home, he was remote and preoccupied. Jack felt invisible. He was largely unaware of how his experiences with his mother and father had affected his reactions to Jennie, but to me it was clear: when he raged at Jennie, he had her full attention. His rage made him feel powerful instead of helpless. Jack and Jennie's negative cycle was a response to the way they had related to their own families. Rage was a safe way to connect, and it was all they knew.

FINDING A WAY THROUGH

All efforts to eliminate rage will fail until its cause is determined. There's an increasingly popular approach to modern medicine known as "functional medicine." The focus of functional medicine is to search for the cause of the illness, as opposed to treating symptoms only, so the cure will be lasting. It's the same in psychology. Unless the cause of a behavior is determined, it will persist. While treating depression, anxiety, poor self-esteem, and relationship problems, we often find that shame is the core issue. But since shame is so heavily defended, it can be quite a challenge to find the core issues.

Importantly, we first need to know what happened to us and then we need to make important distinctions between our experience and who we are. This is the first stage of rectifying shame's distortions and becoming our true self. We must also understand what constitutes realistic expectations for ourselves and others. Can we get our needs met so we can feel filled up inside? This can be a very complex process, best done with another person—a mate, mentor, or therapist. If we didn't get from our parents a dialogue about feelings, needs, and realistic expectations, how are we to know what they are?

Letting Go of Entitlement

Entitlement is the key that unlocks the door to shame and rage. It is not so much a thought process as it is a defensive/reactive state. It's the conduit that anger and rage run through. It's the feeling of an eye for an eye and a tooth for a tooth: *You hurt me so I'm going to hurt you.* Entitlement is at the heart of most dysfunctional couple conflict, so understanding entitlement is the first step to breaking down unproductive conflicts.

So much domestic violence is based on entitlement to rage. To deconstruct entitlement is difficult because of the power that our unconscious process holds over our behavior. The rage response overrules any conscious thought, in spite of our best intentions. The most important part of letting go of entitlement is to embrace the *need* to let it go. We need to completely accept our problem with rage. Then we need to heal the wound at the core of the rage, which is shame. To heal this wound, we need to define ourselves differently—as adequate instead of worthless, empowered instead of weak.

Most people don't understand how their defenses work because they can't see them. If we feel attacked, we defend. It's difficult to remain calm and think of a positive way to respond when we feel hurt by someone we love. Instead, if we are deeply wounded, we are flooded with rage. In all of us the first reaction is to strike back. The righteousness of entitlement is potent and engaging. The only way that I know of to change entitlement is to change the cause. Entitlement is not the problem, shame is. Healing shame must be an ongoing process to correct what is deeply untrue.

Shame can be either intellectual or emotional or both. To heal it we must be aware of it at all times. Then when it expresses itself we must neutralize it by firmly affixing reality thinking to the distortion. The most difficult part of this task is to know what reality is. That takes discussion with others to understand. Asking our mate, our elders, our therapist about what is real is the key to helping ourselves.

The Steps to Understanding Anger and Rage

- Look, see, and understand the way your internal shame system affects your behavior.

- Remember that the cure for shame is to find compassion, understanding, respect, and empathy for yourself and others.

- Learn how to distinguish your real self from the distorted, inadequate self.

- Separate your personal myth (weak, worthless, inadequate) from the way you act and think.

- Learn how to relieve yourself of self-blame by using positive self-talk.

- Know that all change comes from your willingness to look at yourself from the perspective of the other.

- Develop the ability to understand and rectify your relationship distortions as the key that unlocks the door to creating a lasting intimacy.

- Remember that if you live in a state of denial (and the denial of your denial), you will remain locked in the entitlement chamber of rage.

- Find a mentor or enlist your mate as a helper in this process.

Recovering the True Self

Once you completely get the idea that what is actually wrong with you is that you *think* something is wrong with you, then you can start to work on neutralizing the distortion. The steps to neutralizing negative personal myths are to think first about what your myth is telling you, then about what the reality is, and then about what you need to do to fit your negative thinking into your sense of what is real. First, you need to consider what is actually true about who you are: perhaps you are well-meaning, you care about people, or you try to do what is helpful. Then you can begin to separate the truth from the mythic fiction.

You can use self-talk not only to articulate a damaging personal myth but also to debunk it. Let's take a typical personal myth: *No one is going to like me at this party.* You might say to yourself, "That's not true. It is not up to me, it is up to them to decide if they like me. What I can do is to be who I am and see what happens." Self-talk should be tailored to fit your particular self-distortion. You can try out different ideas and concepts to see which one works best. I remember one morning saying to myself, "All I can do is all I can do," and finding this to be a great relief to my worry that my practice would somehow disappear.

Moving Toward the Truth

Ben's parents, Holocaust survivors, were continually terrified and anxious, so much so that they could not provide the emotional support or nurturing that young Ben needed. They worked long hours and were frequently too exhausted to pay much attention to him. He eventually came to the realization that being a good boy, always helping, and being perfect were the best ways to get attention and approval—the closest thing to love that his emotionally shut-down parents could offer. Ben resented his own need for affection because his parents were not able to give it. He felt *humiliated* by his desire for love. And he was enraged that his needs were of so little concern to his parents. In his child's mind, he could not comprehend that his parents were too traumatized and tired to give him the love he craved. Underneath the good boy was an angry, sometimes raging child.

Susan's father was a successful businessman who was seldom home. When he was, the house was filled with unreasonable expectations and anger. Her mother eventually found solace in alcohol and prescription drugs. Susan, like Ben, tried to be a perfect child to please her father and to keep her mother from turning to drugs. Her anger at her parents had to be withdrawn if she was to receive what little affection and attention there was to go around. On the surface she was very nice, but repressed rage was seething underneath.

Ben and Susan entered therapy in crisis. When I asked Ben about his childhood, he said he couldn't remember much of it. But he eventually began to describe a life of loneliness and heartache. He detailed his efforts to be a good son. His compassion for his parents' plight and his devaluation of his own needs for love and affection created an internal wall. Later, when Ben was in college, his repressed neediness caused him to chase after women to get them to want him. When they did, he rejected them, devaluing them for being inferior and stupid. The shame that was linked to Ben's needs caused him to devalue others so he didn't have to feel the pain.

When Ben and Susan began dating, they put on the good-girl and good-boy behaviors they had mastered as children. But after they married, the rage below the surface blew open. They were shaken by the intensity of their tempers. When they first entered therapy, they described a scene where Susan had promised Ben a romantic candlelit dinner, but when he arrived home she was sitting on the sofa chatting with a friend. Ben felt humiliated; it was clear to him that she did not care about him. He fumed until the friend left and then flew into a rage, yelling, "How dare you!" Susan couldn't believe that her husband was reacting this way over a friend coming over and dinner being late. She retaliated, "Are you crazy?" Ben went on yelling: "You don't give a damn about anyone but yourself." He began berating Susan with a laundry list of injustices, and then she lunged at him. The flailing and screaming that ensued caused the neighbors to call the police.

When their marriage was shattered by rage, they could see that something disturbing and powerful was happening. They needed to understand how it worked if they were ever to have a healthy relationship. In the beginning of our therapy we focused on understanding that their behavior—their criticizing and blaming, to which they both felt entitled—was causing substantial emotional pain for both of them. We embarked on a search to find the source of the rage. We discovered that their rage was related to their mutual sense of insignificance, their shared distortion that arose from their early shame.

Ben and Susan worked out some interventions that helped them bring their past issues into the present, where they could talk about them. They began by practicing time-outs when they became angry. Then they created a strategy that included reflecting on the principle they were trying to talk about without getting bogged down in who'd said what to whom. They tried to talk about what they wanted in the future from each other and to think about what personal issues were being stimulated during disagreements. They considered empathy when they worked on a conflict. They learned to check out and verbalize their negative fantasies and then work toward understanding what was happening in real time. In this way they began to learn how to steer clear of behaviors that triggered their rage.

We live in a sea of challenges to our sense of well-being: emotional systems linked to multilayered experiences mixed with impulses like need, sexuality, and hunger, all swimming with thoughts, desire, and fear. When we add another person to the mix, we are in deeper waters than ever. To make matters even more complicated, we develop moral and ethical positions, defenses, and complex relationships running parallel and entwined with each other. This intricate set of impulses, reactions, thoughts, and impressions forms our inner world. All of these processes influence our personality and mood. Our smart defenses can easily trick us into thinking that something we believe to be true is not. The ability of our survival system to develop incredible rationales, to form complex defenses, and then to make us so totally believe in them is truly astounding and deeply human.

To join our personality with another and to develop and maintain a loving relationship can be the rewarding work of a lifetime. The goal is to determine who we are and what we want through examination of the truth that lies within, using the tools that are right in front of us. The poet, psychoanalyst, and post-trauma specialist Clarissa Pinkola Estes writes that "even raw and messy emotions can be understood as a form of light, crackling and bursting with energy. We can use the light of rage in a positive way, in order to see into places we cannot usually see."

For Your Inter-Reflection

Shame, Rage, and Myths of the Self

1. What are you ashamed of about yourself? Do you feel powerless, weak, worthless, bad, or "less than"? Think about how these feelings show up in your relationship and what you do to defend yourself.

2. How do you think understanding your shame issues could affect the way you interact with your partner?

3. What are the most important emotional understandings you need from your partner?

4. What can you tell your partner about how to support you when you are mad, sad, or needy?

5. When you find yourself taking something personally, needing to be right, or getting defensive, what can you do to calm down, look at it another way, or give yourself a break?

intimacy and the art of love

The married are those who have taken the terrible risk of intimacy and, having taken it, know life without intimacy to be impossible.

—Carolyn Heilbrun

FOR MOST OF US, THE WORD *intimate* conjures up romantic images of candlelit dinners, slow dancing, and long passionate kisses. Romantic gestures are certainly a dominant theme of intimacy, but there is more. Intimacy in the real world is the result of expressing our feelings, our personal secrets, and our deepest truths to each other. It arises when we feel cared about, accepted, and loved for our own sake, warts and all.

The word intimacy originates from the Latin word *intima*, which means "inner" or "innermost." Thomas Patrick Malone writes in *The Art of Intimacy*, "The outstanding quality of the intimate experience is the sense of *being in touch with* our real selves. It allows us a fresh awareness of who, what, and how we are."

THE ELEMENTS OF INTIMACY

Ideally, intimacy is a blend of emotional closeness, spiritual connectedness, and an open heart and mind. Its origin lies in intellectual collaboration and familiarity, especially with one another's culture and interests. It may also involve shared religious or philosophical beliefs. Finally, intimacy can be an emotional response to knowing someone well by virtue of shared experiences. When we think of the word *intimate* we see both the word *in* and the word *mate*. That is kind of how it works: being inside another person in a way that feels as though we psychologically mate with him or her and in that way become *intimate*.

When we share details about our life that usually remain hidden, we are connecting in an intimate way. The extent to which we can disclose deeply private personal feelings and experiences is proportionate to how safe we feel, so safety is a requirement for intimacy as well. Of course, intimacy means different things to different people, and its meaning for us may even change over time. It can be linked with sexual closeness, but not necessarily; intimate feelings arise from shared moments of emotional connection as well as from sexual encounters. Whatever its particular nature, intimacy is the product of relationship work and the result of feeling emotionally connected to our loved one. It's the operating principle for creating love.

The Inner World

As Thomas Patrick Malone eloquently makes clear, intimacy is not only about the other, it is about *who we are*. And the most powerful and profound awareness of who we are comes when we open our hearts to others, allowing them to touch our deepest sensitivity. In the act of risking our tender inner world, we become more of who we are because we feel touched in an untouched place.

Intimacy takes courage because we must risk expressing our deepest sense of self to create it. We may be apprehensive about opening our hearts and minds to another for fear of being judged or rejected. But the reward is immense. It is the antidote to painful aloneness. It reaches into our hearts, providing love that satisfies our need for emotional food. Our ability to establish and maintain nurturing intimate relationships is not only gratifying, it nourishes us and ultimately helps keep us sane.

Our survival as a species requires that we seek connections with others and open our own inner world to them. Intimacy breaks into our isolation and intertwines our souls and, if done with tenderness and care, creates safe and secure attachments. This ability to intimately connect with others is the backbone of civilization. Intimacy is what makes us human.

Psychotherapy and Intimacy

What does psychotherapy have to do with intimacy? The connection is in its process. The practice of face-to-face talk therapy is essentially intimate. In the psychotherapeutic setting we are encouraged to talk freely, to open up our mind and heart and find understanding and compassion in response. When therapy works, it's because it operates as a model for how intimate interaction can work in the outside world. Many times people coming into therapy have never had an intimate relationship and are scared to death of it. In a safe setting they can experiment with ideas, express feelings, and talk about what matters to them without judgment or criticism. The one-way quality of the intimate setting helps them experience what it means to be close to and known by another without the fear or the burden of having to know that person in return. This kind of safety is the quality of good parenting that very young children need to develop properly. In this sense, psychotherapy is a creation of the intimacy that is often missed in childhood—a way for patients to have an experience of intimacy that they have never had.

Self and Other

There are two major components to feeling intimate. First there is intimacy with ourselves: the personal intimacy that comes from being familiar with our own inner truths, our dreams, beliefs, feelings, thoughts, wishes, and desires. Second, there is intimacy with our partner: the connection we cultivate when we bring this personal process into our primary relationship. This model for relationship intimacy includes emotional availability, empathy, caretaking, tender responsiveness, and bearing ambivalence during difficult times. How we are with ourselves and how we relate to our partner is a critical part of the dance between our inner and outer worlds, an interplay that can either enhance or inhibit our capacity to be happy together.

Intimate activity can take many forms, from giving each other the freedom to explore individual interests to developing mutual values, hopes, and dreams. Intimacy that is created from an open dialogue about our inner and outer worlds ultimately teaches us about ourselves and who we are as people. As we develop a language for our relationship by expressing our feelings and thoughts, we meld our two separate worlds into one whole.

A loving relationship arises from attending to our own thoughts and feelings and to those of our partner. From this process we produce shared values, beliefs, feelings, and interests. To reveal our true self in the presence of another in this way, if done with care, can be enlivening, enlightening, and joyful. What could be more satisfying than understanding with greater compassion because we know someone better? But to achieve this kind of contentment both in our relationship and within ourselves involves an evolution of understanding. It is a process, not a short-term goal. We hear the adage that it's not the destination that counts, but the journey. There is no point where we have "arrived," but a real sense of moving up a very long stream. Harmony comes from shining insight into dark places along the way, and with that light removing obstructions that block our ability to love deeply and intimately.

THE ARCHITECTURE OF LOVE

Creating intimacy is a lot like building a house. We start with a solid foundation of truth, acceptance, and reality; we lay out the rooms of our desires, fantasies, wants, and needs; we frame the windows to our soul, wire in our emotional connections, add the hardware of values, joy, and sexuality, and join them all together to create a home. The raw materials for our building are drawn from a dialogue about what we want, need, and value about ourselves and our mate.

The dialogue of intimacy, as we've seen, is about knowing who we are and what we want from life together and making agreements based on realistic expectations and shared values. To keep the dialogue open and constructive, it's helpful to keep some key points in mind:

- **Understand your fears so they don't come out as blame or criticism.** If we are afraid to be close for fear of rejection, or if we feel ashamed about needing anyone, we may use blame and criticism to distance ourselves as a protective measure.

- **Acknowledge what your partner is telling you before you make your point.** Letting our partner know that we understand how he or she feels maintains our connection.

- **Discuss what you want and need from each other.** Defining our needs helps us know more about how to satisfy them. It is also a way to work through the fear of depending on or needing anyone.

- **Build commonality through conversations about deeply held beliefs.** Making connections through common values and concerns helps to build a stronger base.

- **Air complaints on a regular basis.** Don't let them build up too long or they will create resentment and distance.

- **Be in touch with your defensiveness so you can prevent it from disrupting your ability to solve problems.** The more we know about how our defenses are working, the better able we are to prevent emotional distance. By being unable to listen and respond to what our partner is trying to tell us, we impede our ability to resolve conflicts.

- **Never assume.** People often act on assumptions without ever giving the other person the right to deny them or correct them. Assumptions are often about our own issues that we are projecting onto our partner. Check out your assumptions by asking about them in the form of a question, such as: "When we were talking the other night about my past, it felt like you were being critical of me, even though you didn't say it directly. Did you mean to be critical?"

- **Treat your partner with respect.** Be civil and listen with an open mind.

Listening at the Door

One of the most important things we can do to develop intimacy is to learn how to listen well to what our partner is trying to tell us. If intimacy is like a house, we might say that listening is the door by which we enter. And active listening is more than hearing what our mate has to say; it's letting him or her know that we have heard and giving feedback that validates what's been said. Let's say our mate wants to talk about a bad day at work. We can listen actively using simple responses: nodding, saying "Yes" or "Uh-huh," or actually repeating back what we have heard ("It sounds like your boss said some harsh things in that meeting").

Intimacy stimulates an entire range of feelings and moods. In healthy relationships, feelings may fluctuate from being in love to feeling annoyance or anger to not feeling much of anything. Life stresses such as work pressures, health issues, family crises, and difficulties with friends affect our mood states, evoking emotional responses. If we are to live in harmony with our partner, we need to be aware of how our fluctuating feelings affect our ability to love.

Mood changes within a relationship are not necessarily indications of psychological ill health. Troubling life issues stimulate our emotional memories, thus creating our moods. *The truth is that there is no cure for life.* We will all experience death; we will all have physical infirmities, losses, and painful remembrances from our past. Developing an awareness of the variations in emotions from day to day helps us to form realistic expectations for our relationship. We cannot be eternally cheery and fun-loving. We are all plagued by dark moods and anxious moments at times. If this becomes a part of our shared reality, we can provide a space to work on it instead of taking it personally.

So what can we do about those fluctuations? Sometimes the best thing to do is nothing; just let the mood pass. Give your partner space to work through his or her mood, but when he or she does want to talk, be available to listen. Include feelings and moods in your dialogue with each other, and learn to make room for both of you in your discussions.

Through the Looking Glass

The most common mistake that couples make is to miss the emotional component in a discussion or a conflict. We can avoid this pitfall by using the active-listening technique called mirroring—a way of reflecting back not the literal but the emotional content of what we've heard: "You must feel terrible about what your boss said to you." Offering solutions doesn't work unless we are specifically asked for them. When our partner is telling us about a bad day, it is probably not the best time to explain why we think he's having one.

Active listening is about active empathy. Empathy is putting ourselves in the other person's shoes or seeing things through her eyes. Heinz Kohut, who developed a school of psychology called Self Psychology, defined empathy as "vicarious introspection," which is the ability to vicariously imagine and feel the experience of the other. True empathy is a bridge to another person's mind and heart. Active empathy is especially important in conflicts, which often escalate because neither person is listening to what's really being said—because they are not reaching each other across that bridge. The most common mistake that couples make is to miss the emotional component in a discussion or a conflict. By empathically tuning in to the sounds of the heart, we can create closeness even during conflicts.

Learning from Our Defenses

Expressing what is in our hearts, with compassion, empathy, and a willingness to listen, is one of the most fundamental techniques of building intimacy. But there are other factors that impede our ability to love deeply—that keep our "house" from being as structurally sound and warmly welcoming as it could be. First, we all fear loss, humiliation, abandonment, and death. Second, we defend against those conditions. Third, the greater the pain that's associated with the condition, the fiercer the defense will be.

The defenses our mind automatically creates will even distort reality to protect us from pain. Like an odorless, tasteless gas, they can color our psychological point of view to create states of mind in which others may appear highly attractive and available or stale and lifeless. The survival part of our brain will do whatever it takes to protect us from the possibility of being hurt, especially if a present threat reminds us of an earlier trauma. So our defenses work to protect us. We may no longer need the protection, but we are not consciously aware of that.

The Secret Life of Fear

When people become fearful, they may direct it outward by criticizing and blaming their partners for what they are experiencing. This causes an emotional disconnect. But there is a way for couples to communicate about fear that can strengthen their connection. For example, I was working with a couple who were contemplating having another child. Luke, an architect, criticized and blamed his wife, Amanda, a stay-at-home mother caring for their two small children, for their money problems. Instead of telling her how afraid he was of being the sole breadwinner, he defended against being exposed and then feeling humiliated by criticizing her for spending too much money and being generally irresponsible. Feeling wounded, she would shoot back with a criticism about his inability to make enough money. Their interchanges grew more and more angry and bitter.

When Luke and Amanda began therapy, they were cycling round and round in a spate of criticism and defensiveness. Slowly, over time, Luke began to see that his criticism of his wife was actually about his fear of not being strong enough to handle the responsibility of a wife and child—having another child might mean he would fail and then lose her. He finally marshaled his courage and told her that he was afraid that the additional responsibility was too much for him and that his stress and anxiety might erode their marriage. Amanda, for her part, wanted the kind of happy family life she never had. Her fear was that Luke didn't want her enough to care about her desire to have children. But once she knew what was bothering him, she felt more compassionate and loving. She realized that they had to work together to help each other with the strain that another child would bring into the marriage.

When we explore what our defenses are telling us about our fear, guilt, and shame, we build bridges to reality from our deepest mythology. As we distinguish what is real from what we fear is real, we are building a healthier connection with our mate. In this way we can stay in contact with our true self. It is reality carved from essential personal dialogue that is the building block of communication and loving insight. Eliminating fear is part of the natural dance of intimacy.

BOUNDARIES? WHAT BOUNDARIES?

What do boundary issues have to do with intimacy? Generally, boundaries delineate interpersonal space, which can be either physical or emotional. Physical space means how much physical distance between us and how much time alone we need for our well-being. Emotional space is about being able to express what we need and want both individually and with our mate. Emotional space is actually about our feelings. Understanding what our feelings are telling us about what is comfortable and what is not helps us to define our boundaries. Feelings help us to define our own place in the world so other people's needs don't crowd out our own. Otherwise we become overburdened and end up not taking good care of ourselves, which makes us depressed. Setting boundaries is a good way to express how we feel and what we want.

We learn how to understand what our feelings mean from our parents. When parents take the time to help their children define

The Royal Road to Intimacy

- Discuss and define realistic expectations.

- Make time to talk. Include your fears and worries as well as your hopes and dreams.

- Explore what you can do to help your partner with the things that are important to him or her.

- Express physical affection regularly.

- Make eye contact when you talk.

- Promote psychological, physical, and emotional safety.

- Create a regular time alone together with no distractions.

- Ask for what you want.

- Express your truth with compassion.

- Take responsibility for your part in relationship and personal problems.

- Stop and listen to what your partner thinks and feels.

- Live in the present and promote a positive future together.

- Write a love letter expressing all the things that you love about your partner.

- Write a letter of apology for all the things that you have done to hurt him or her.

- Trade letters.

what their feelings mean, they build a vocabulary of emotions that they can use to draw boundaries. Let's say a child is crying. If the parent talks to the child about what is going on—"You are sad because your friend can't come over to play today"—the child begins to make connections between sad feelings and external events. Without this information it can be quite difficult to set boundaries as an adult.

I often tell patients that the best reason not to do something is because they don't want to or it doesn't feel good to them. If we are hungry, we ask our stomach what it wants. If we feel sad, happy, or bad about something, we should ask our feelings what they mean and then decide what we want to do about it.

Defending the Borders

We naturally feel like moving closer to someone if it feels comfortable to be with him or her; we tend to move away if it doesn't. In his song "50 Ways to Leave Your Lover," Paul Simon opines, "Slip out the back, Jack / Make a new plan, Stan." This is the feeling that comes over us when we can't establish proper physical or emotional boundaries. Even if we don't literally slip out the back, we find other ways—such as being passive or distracted, creating conflict, or working unnecessarily long hours to avoid dealing with issues—to put space between us and our partner if we cannot articulate what we need. Often people who live alone do so because they can't set boundaries.

Setting Positive Boundaries

A positive process for establishing boundaries depends on a clear sense of our feelings, needs, and wants as well as what feels right for our partner. To be true to ourselves is to be true to our own personal space. Compromises need to be made, of course, and finding the spot where each person feels comfortable is the eventual goal.

Most people have their own fixed preferences about personal boundaries, but it takes some processing with our mate to agree on boundary issues within a relationship. "Boundary issues" may include feeling pressured for connection, affection, sex, or intimacy when we don't feel ready for it. Frequently, in the early stages of romantic life, couples are joined at the hip. The initial intensity of desire and fear of loss binds them physically together. After some time, they begin to feel the need for some physical or emotional space to engage in personally satisfying activities. Meeting this need requires both the ability to sense it and the ability to articulate it.

Discussions about boundaries can help couples bypass potential conflicts. In fact, the discussion itself often serves the purpose of setting firm and healthy boundaries. There is no buzzer that sounds when a boundary has been crossed; we have to understand what boundaries mean, both within ourselves and between each other, to create a sense of safety. If we cannot establish a way to communicate our needs to each other, then we may risk violating a boundary. When we step over our partner's boundaries, we may find him or her in a fight-or-flight reaction, and an argument or distance will result. If we can't say no when we need to, then it will be difficult to be close for fear of losing ourselves altogether. If we set boundaries on a regular basis, though, we feel more comfortable.

Here are some statements that you can use to discuss boundaries with your partner when you feel the need to do so. Importantly, this process requires that you check into what your feelings and your body are telling you about what you need and want in order to gain emotional balance.

- "I need some alone time."

- "This is as much closeness as I can manage for right now."

- "Let me know when you want some physical or emotional space."

- "I'm not feeling well; I need you to help me."

- "Your body language is telling me what you want, but I need your words."

- "Please ask me when you want to borrow something of mine."

Home on the Range

Jon's wife, Joan, owned several horses, and whenever she could get away she would go out to visit them at the ranch where they were boarded. Jon had grown up on a ranch with horses and ridden often while growing up. To him horses were a mode of transportation, adventure, and fun, rather than a lifestyle. Joan, on the other hand, had bought her first horse as an adult. She loved the work of owning horses, not just riding, training, grooming, and attending horse shows, but the friends and the life of being outdoors.

On one particular Saturday, after a long and difficult week, both Jon and Joan were feeling tired and edgy on their way out to the ranch. Jon's agenda was to go on a trail ride and chill out, but Joan wanted to do chores and work around the stalls. When they arrived, she promptly read him her list of things that had to be done. By the time she had reached item six, Jon could feel himself getting tense. Wanting to be a good sport, he went along with her agenda, but inside he was seething.

As they were driving home, Joan cautioned Jon to slow down because there were dogs in the area that could run out into the road. He replied tersely that she was picking on him. This triggered a defensive reaction from Joan, and they began to argue. Jon had come along to relax and instead there was tension. What were they not seeing?

As they drove, they sat quietly so they could cool off from the confrontation about Jon's driving and what had built up during the day. After about 20 minutes of silence, their anger subsided and they began to talk things through. Jon acknowledged his agenda, his fatigue, and his inability to talk about it. Joan talked about her stress and her need to get so much done. They tried to understand what their basic conflict was about. Jon explained that he was especially sensitive to the way Joan asked him to do things. He discussed how her intensity was difficult for him when he felt stressed. This unraveling was crucial. They started off talking about what they were going through instead of blaming or criticizing each other. By explaining what they were experiencing, they were building empathy and compassion for each other's personal struggles that day, and this was a good way of working through their underlying issues.

Jon's father was authoritarian and controlling. He frequently ordered Jon around, had him work endless hours, and made him feel like a slave. So when Joan gave Jon orders, it opened an old wound. Not only did his father never take the time to explain to Jon what Jon's feelings might be telling him about what he did and didn't want, he never allowed Jon to express his feelings at all. So here Jon was at the ranch, having a very difficult time laying out his needs and wants and therefore his boundaries, but getting angry with Joan because he couldn't do it.

Joan hadn't understood this. Her intention had only been to get some work done, and she thought Jon was just being very reactive. Joan herself had also grown up feeling controlled. Now that she was an adult, the ranch was her place to be in charge. She was unaware of how her behavior was affecting Jon.

As they began to understand what was going on, many of the complex underpinnings of this conflict became clear. They expressed and acknowledged their needs and complaints. From their discussion about what they needed from each other and what they wanted for themselves, they came to understand their boundaries and agree on them. They felt better understood, safer, and therefore more intimate. The key factor was their willingness to calmly and thoughtfully go through their experience together until they'd spelled out the experience in a way they could both grasp.

Jon and Joan were building and preserving intimacy because:

- Neither one withdrew or became critical, defensive, controlling, or contemptuous.

- They listened to each other until they understood each other's position.

- They went deeper to see the source of the pain.

- They concentrated on their mutual wants, needs, and feelings to define comfortable boundaries with each other.

- They made a plan for next time.

We've seen that intimacy is critical to making love last, and we've looked at some of the qualities and behaviors that support lasting intimacy. In the rest of this chapter, we'll explore some common—and daunting—obstructions to our ability to be intimate and to love freely.

OVERCOMING BARRIERS TO INTIMACY

Love brings forth our entire emotional experience, as we've seen, and this naturally includes our personal pain. For those of us

What Keeps Partners Apart?

- Inattention to each other and the relationship.

- Lack of respect for each other.

- Lack of tenderness toward each other.

- Lack of physical contact or eye contact.

- Verbal, physical, or emotional abuse.

- Inability to express feelings.

- Not making time for each other.

- Unspoken or unresolved anger and resentment; avoiding confrontation.

- Unrealistic expectations.

- Inability to articulate wants and needs.

- Being too compliant; saying what you think your partner wants to hear.

- Deception, dishonesty, or game-playing.

- Thinking that you can change your partner.

- Blaming, shaming, criticizing, and judging.

- Acting like the victim instead of the problem solver.

- Being unwilling to look into family issues as a source of current issues.

- Being unable or unwilling to work out the past.

- Bringing up the past as a way to avoid living in the present.

- Assuming that you know what your partner thinks and feels.

who have felt the sting of rejection, loss, or abandonment, loving someone creates a certain amount of distress. The urge to possess the other so we can keep ourselves safe from rejection can be strong, even bordering on obsession. The paradox of love is that we want to possess the desire of the other—want them to love us as we love them—yet this same urge to possess them can drive them away. Our need to control the relationship, arising from our dread of being abandoned or humiliated, can strangle love or kill it from within. Intimacy is extinguished in this self-saving secret process of holding in. It is like we are being pulled along by powerful internal memories that we are only dimly aware of. Our fears, obsessions, drives, and urges are part of who we are. To keep these processes secret creates separateness and produces behaviors that may appear as defenses. To create an intimate attachment is to connect to these dark feelings, understand their meaning, and allow them to lead us toward an intimate connection with our loved one. To bring out the underpinnings of our worst fear may allow us to be not only truly seen, but accepted. In this way we heal our pain as we open our heart.

Carl Jung said, "Where love rules, there is no will to power; and where power predominates, there love is lacking. The one is the shadow of the other." In relationships, control is the ultimate power tool, and being perfect is just one way of exerting control. Attempting to be perfect—to control our own personalities—is an effort to control how others see us; it's how we hide our inadequacy. But what causes someone to want to control someone else? Is it really an attempt to control one's *own* internal life? Can we say that controlling the external world acts as an internal control? If we look at controlling behavior from a logical point of view, we can see that it's meant to keep what feels out of control from going that way. Trying to control the outside world is an attempt to stabilize our inner world. Controlling others is a way to control our own fear of falling apart or losing ourselves altogether.

Some Theories about Control Issues

Control issues in adulthood begin with early power struggles that were lost to an overbearing parent, leaving the child feeling powerless and invisible. These early losses robbed the child of control. When a parent controls his or her child completely, there can be no equality or true relationship. The child's will is squelched. The parent's needs have prevailed over the child's own. It's the parent's job to help the child develop self-control, learn how to soothe himself, and express and satisfy basic needs. This skill gives the child mastery over his behavior. If the parent is the source of control, the child never learns how to maintain his own equilibrium. He is forced into isolation, unable to process anxiety or pain on his own and deprived of the chance to do so with a nurturing parent instead of an overbearing or controlling one. And when this child grows into adulthood, still lacking the ability to process anxiety and pain, the only option available to him is to control the outside world as much as possible. If we have no internal mechanism for controlling our internal fears, anxiety, or pain, we must exert control over our environment so that we don't stimulate these internally painful and chaotic states. This means that we seek to control others as a means of controlling our internal world. The conflict this creates can be enormous.

Parents who are critical and distant toward their children inadvertently lead them to the same solution: *be perfect*. Perfectionism is a reaction that all children have to abuse, criticism, and distance from parents. The child attempts to both avoid pain and bring the parent close by being better, more perfect. The problem with this condition is that it creates self-criticism, high expectations, and a false sense of self. In effect, the child idealizes the parent while devaluing the self. Later on, in relationships, this creates depression, high expectations for self and others, and a hidden inadequate self. So the controlling parent creates a controlling adult. In adult relationships, controlling partners create tension, distance, and resentment. Their need to control the environment around them only establishes distance, because controlling the outside world helps to soothe them inside but makes no room for the other person.

All children *identify* as a precursor to *identity*. It is the way we learn how to talk, walk, eat, develop social skills, and so on. So we also identify with the critical parent and take him or her in as a part of how we relate to ourselves. The perfectionistic child is constantly failing to be perfect and criticizing herself for it. As she identifies with the parent, so will she connect her anger with her parent's criticism, and this will become her critical inner voice. This internal aggression makes it impossible for the child, and later the adult, to feel self-accepting or to successfully self-soothe. It drives her to look outside herself for comforting and approval—first toward her parents and later toward others—for acceptance, nurturing, inner peace, and stability. In this way the perfectionist becomes a people-pleaser to gain the equilibrium that is lacking within.

Perfectionistic behavior that aims to create closeness by approval-seeking instead creates distance. The work we do to be perfect does not allow us to disclose our true self; every move must be measured against the ideal perfect self. We want others to praise us so we can feel better inside, but the inevitable outcome is alienation. The drive for perfection pulls us into ourselves to fix what feels defective. We want to make ourselves perfect both so our flaws won't show and so others won't withdraw from us as our parents did. Our efforts to gain closeness fail because we must focus inward to hide our imperfections and therefore cannot connect with others in a real way. We can easily see how this process would affect intimacy: we may appear to be nice on the outside, even perfect, but inwardly we may be secretly angry. This anger could be expressed through emotional distance, perhaps perceived as coldness, or it could be expressed in a huge outburst, or through passive behaviors that anger our partner, like being late or forgetting important things.

Perfectionism is essentially inauthentic because we must hide our true self in favor of a false self that is sculpted to fit every situation. These behaviors are not bad or wrong; they are intended to get needs met and to maintain internal equilibrium. But they cannot give us what we truly need. When couples encounter perfection and control, it's a clear indicator that they are looking to their relationship to do something that they are unable to do for themselves. We all need to feel accepted but if we try to get others to do that for us, we end up becoming even more cut off and alone. Taking control of our need for self-acceptance allows us to forget ourselves and focus on the other. In this way we can find the kind of quality connection we are yearning for.

Losing the Perfect Addiction

So how do we shift our focus? Recognizing that we have a need for control is the first step. Seeing what we need from others and what we must do for ourselves is the second step. This revolves around the distinction between self and other: What we need from ourselves is self-acceptance, interests, something to devote ourselves to that we personally enjoy, healthy self-esteem, and true comfort in our own skin. What we intrinsically need from others is love, nurturing, affection, sex, and companionship. The third step is to understand our history and how it has affected the way we get our needs met. Trying to get our needs met by being perfect is never a good solution; we have to give too much of ourselves away to get much in return. What's more, our own sense of perfection, with its self-critical underbelly, will destroy affectionate comments before they can do any good. The last step, a very important step, is to learn how to nurture ourselves. Nurturing ourselves means that we do things like take good care of ourselves, be kind to ourselves, maintain our health, and find time to enjoy pursuits that make us feel good about who we are. Following these steps can be a good guide for keeping us on track and not overburdening our relationship.

People do not decide to behave badly. They behave badly because they're afraid and in a great deal of emotional pain. Behavior has logic to it; it's *about* something, or it wouldn't be there. So how can we find out what that something is? A good place to look for answers is within ourselves—literally, within our own body. The body doesn't lie, it can only feel. Lying requires thinking, and the body doesn't think, it simply reacts; it just is.

Trusting the Body

As we saw earlier when we talked about building an emotional vocabulary based on feelings, needs, and desire, we need to know what our feelings are telling us, not only to form better boundaries but to communicate our reactions. Only then can we find a way to convey important emotional information to our partner. The goal is to discover the reasons why we feel as we do and develop a vocabulary for expressing those needs and feelings from the information that our body is sending us. When we are small and something happens to us that causes us to feel sad or scared, our parents or caretakers articulate what our feelings mean to us. Something like: "You are sad because I haven't been home this week to help you go to sleep." These descriptions from parents give children a vocabulary for their feelings. These early experiences help children to know more about what they want and need. If we don't have experiences like this, we will not understand much of what our feelings are telling us about what we are experiencing. It then becomes much more difficult as adults to form boundaries or communicate with our partner what we feel, want, or don't want.

Our body is a good resource because it just reacts, whereas our mind is always trying to help us out by forming defenses and rationalizations for our behavior. Developing the ability to express feelings or needs requires that we know what our body is telling us. So we need to find some method for processing this information—through therapy, or with help from our mate, or by listening and reflecting on our own.

Start with these steps:

- Take time to listen to your body. Think about what is happening with it. Do you feel tension, bad feelings, sadness, knots in your stomach? Ask yourself what these feelings are about. Do they remind you of any experience from your past that you can identify?

- Understand that you have a right to talk about how you feel and what your boundaries are, no matter what. It doesn't mean your feelings are necessarily rational, but they have a right to exist.

- Know that all feelings are responses both to the present and to the past in some way. It is important to understand the connection. If you were abandoned, criticized, or abused in the past, you will overreact to the same condition in the present or build defenses.

- If you find yourself angry, blaming, critical, or defensive, take a look at what might be underneath the feeling.

What We Owe Ourselves

In finding out what our feelings are telling us about how we are experiencing our partner, there is a need to understand what happens inside each of us and between us—our history, our internal life, and how these merge with our partner's. The idea is to balance our precious connection to another person with a healthy internal life. When couples are caught up in a negative cycle of criticism and defense, it is because they either don't understand what they are feeling and needing or don't trust each other with the truth.

Not every feeling or need can be met in real life. There are many things we do because we are obligated to do them. Life is full of obligations, some of them pleasant, most of them unavoidable, like birthdays, weddings, funerals, holidays, religious rituals, business meetings, and regular visits to family. But too many obligations can overburden us, make us feel resentful, and affect our ability to be generous toward ourselves. When our lives are filled to the brim with obligations from work, family, and friends and we believe that we must do whatever is asked or face rejection, we risk losing our connection to who we are. There is a necessary balance between what we need to do for those we love and what we need to do for ourselves. If our personality is formed around pleasing everyone, we will be giving away our ability to make ourselves happy, which is our obligation to ourselves.

To maintain our connection to who we are, it is important to understand that we do not necessarily "owe" everyone else more than we "owe" ourselves. Yes, making others happy can make us happy, but we must strike a balance between what we do for others and what we do for ourselves. To this end, *everyone counts, including us.*

In many cultures the concept of selflessness is held high as a standard of admiration: think of Mother Teresa and Gandhi. But this is an unrealistic expectation for most of us in this modern world. We need to take care of ourselves. The moral precepts of Zen Buddhism instruct us to exercise proper care of the body and the mind. This principle is based on the belief that we are responsible for our well-being. In this way, if we are making ourselves happy, we are giving our good feelings to all those around us. The goal is to find equilibrium between our obligations to others and our need do things that make us feel good about ourselves. Working toward a balanced life is an important value, even if it may be hard to achieve in our hectic lives. Our sense of well-being is one of the best places in life to do the work to maintain an intimate connection with our mate. Being intimate within through knowing how we feel and expressing our needs and wants is critical. But taking good care of ourselves is the best way not to overburden our relationship by expecting our partner to do for us what we are unable to do for ourselves.

Food for Love

So what do relationships have to do with well-being when well-being is something we owe to ourselves? As we mentioned earlier, we need intimacy to feed our soul. Woody Allen sums it up in his tour-de-force film *Annie Hall* when he asks, "Why do we want relationships at all?" He tells a story about his uncle, who, when asked why he dressed up like a chicken, replied, "Because I need the eggs." We need relationships because they are the way we get emotionally fed through nurturing and intimacy. When we accept that we humans are inescapably bound to each other the same way we have been for thousands of years, from tribes to communities to nations, we come to see the value of relationship as our very salvation. Intimacy is our lifeblood; we need it to feel alive and connected to something beyond ourselves. We *do* need the eggs.

Intimacy is the emotional balm for the inescapable entrapment of our own skin. It's our bond with others that enables us to cross over the psychological void of separateness to the world of our loved one in the ephemeral bliss of connectedness. If we are to be intimate, we must open our heart, knowing that we can be hurt, and give of our precious gift, our tender truth, in a moment of being truly vulnerable and alive. To this end we strive and wish and dream.

For Your Inter-Reflection

Intimacy and the Art of Love

1. List the ways you need your partner. Make a distinction between things you need for the health of the relationship and things you need for your own feelings' sake.

2. What does your partner do that touches you most? What do you do when you are most touched?

3. When was the last time your partner hurt you? What was it that hurt and why? Can you talk about it with your partner?

4. Make a list of the feelings you have for your partner and those you had for your parents. Are they the same or different? How so?

5. What are your worst fears in your relationship? Can you talk about them with your partner? Why or why not?

6. What makes you happy with yourself and what makes you happy with your partner?

7. Write a letter of apology to your partner. Then write a love letter. Then write a letter that explains what makes you happy. Share the letters with your partner.

6

how conflict can create love

What cannot be said will get wept.

—Jim Harrison

FALLING IN LOVE IS a truly wonderful experience, but love doesn't stay wonderful all by itself. Continuing to love that same person over time depends on our ability to resolve conflicts that naturally arise. Most relationships fail because couples are not able to resolve conflicts in a healthy way. Couples who blame, criticize, defend, and rage will have great difficulty maintaining intimacy.

Conflict is layered. The first layer is what we observe on the surface. There are often several other layers of emotion, related to our past experiences and ultimately how we feel about ourselves. Conflict taps into our entire personality and stimulates all our defenses. On the positive side, conflict also presents a unique opportunity to both learn about ourselves and, if the conflict is resolved properly, create a deeper intimate connection.

Kenneth Cloke, a skilled mediator (and my brother), writes in his book *The Crossroads of Conflict*:

> Most conflicts are filled with a cacophony of noisome chaos that confuses people about their real meaning. Yet at their

center, as in the eye of a hurricane, there is silence and peace, which poet Rainer Maria Rilke described beautifully as the noise at the entryway to the voiceless silence of a true conflict. When we pay attention to this voiceless silence in conflict—to what people really mean—everything they do or say can lead to the center of their dispute. The parties can locate this center, as with all circles, not by moving outward against their opponents, but by moving inward toward the core of the conflict within themselves.

WHAT MAKES CONNECTIONS AND WHAT BREAKS THEM?

We fade in on a couple sitting quietly at Sunday morning breakfast. Suddenly, a seemingly innocuous comment swiftly shifts the peaceful mood into prodigious conflict.

She: Could you be more careful when you take out the trash? Yesterday you left a total mess.

He (stung): Well, excuse me. I didn't know I was getting the white-glove test.

She (annoyed by his tone): I don't see how you could have missed it. Are you blind?

He: I just can't win. Whatever I do, it's never good enough for you.

She: Well, if you would just open your eyes and pay attention to what you were doing, then I wouldn't have to say anything.

He: There you go, blaming me again. You are such a control freak.

So it goes until they either start yelling or stop talking altogether. All couples experience conflict—but conflict can either break their connection or be the basis for deeper intimacy. Imagine the same conflict expressed in a different way:

She: I want to ask you something, but I don't want you to take it the wrong way. Thank you for taking out the trash, but next time could you please check to see if you left any trash behind? I would really appreciate it.

He: I'm sorry. I was in a hurry and didn't realize that I did that. I'll double-check next time, and thank you for telling me in such a nice way.

We know that kindness, thoughtfulness, concern, and empathy create connections, while criticism, disrespect, defensiveness, and anger disrupt and undermine them. So why is it sometimes so difficult for couples to behave kindly? The simple truth is that the roots of a couple's conflict often run quite deep.

We have all witnessed couples who are quarreling, and their level of criticism, contempt, and defensive behavior makes it clear why they're having trouble. When couples take the gloves off and use words like weapons, they wipe out all the good feelings. They too easily fall into using the same dysfunctional skills they learned in their own families, and they create the same anger and resentment in their current relationship that they felt growing up.

Each person's sense of reality is based on his or her own unique perspective. We are all born with a certain temperament, physical appearance, intelligence, and innate talents. We believe, think, need, care about, are sensitive to, or are wounded by certain experiences, some similar to each other's and some quite different. These diverse traits and experiences form our personality and worldview. When we find that special someone, we are encountering a different set of traits and experiences, forming our partner's particular personality. Where our differences clash, conflicts arise, shaped by our particular patterns of personality and experience.

Conflict is the natural result of our different likes and dislikes, our particular sensitivities, our perceived slights, and our emotional wounds—in short, of our being two diverse people. All couples experience conflict, and accepting that conflict is a natural process is an important step toward creating intimacy. The problem is not *that* we fight, it's *how* we fight. How we respond to conflicts has everything to do with resolving them. Productive and efficient conflict resolution is a vital dynamic in the creation of lasting love. Until we learn this crucial skill, we will find ourselves caught up in the same negative exchanges time and again.

I once worked with a couple in which the husband was angry and bitter toward his wife because she never initiated sex. Of course, his behavior was completely counterproductive: his anger and bitterness made his wife withdraw all the more. As we peeled back the layers, we discovered that he felt truly unlovable. Once he understood where his anger was coming from, he could risk expressing how much he loved and needed his wife. This work helped them forge a deeper bond that in turn led to an improved sexual connection. It just took some digging to ferret out the conflict's source.

THROUGH A GLASS, DARKLY

The little story above, which demonstrates the difficulty couples encounter in their quest for a loving relationship, also shows how hard it can be for them to see what is getting in their way. Our view of what's going on in our relationship, in our partner's mind and heart, and even within ourselves can be so clouded by distorted perceptions and projections that the true nature of our conflict is completely obscured. Let's take a closer look at how this happens and what we can do to see more clearly.

Repression and Projection

Before Brad and Teresa met, they had experienced a wide variety of relationships, all ending somewhat dismally. They were both lonely when they met, so their relationship progressed fast and they soon moved in together. Teresa was thrilled because she felt she had met Mr. Right. Brad seemed to love her in the way she had always wanted. He sent love notes, he hung on her every word, and the sex was off the charts. Everything was on track for marriage.

One day, while they were in a restaurant, out of nowhere Brad flew into a jealous rage. He wanted to know why Teresa was flirting with "that man across the room." When Teresa recovered slightly from her shock and dismay, she explained that she was not looking at anyone, but Brad wouldn't believe her. Their meal was ruined, and the trouble didn't stop there. At home, they fought bitterly about whether Teresa had been flirting or not. She was mystified by Brad's jealousy; she reassured him that she had been waiting for him all her life and that she was completely content with him. But Brad continued to berate her. When nothing would convince him otherwise, they came to my office for help.

Teresa was already coming to me for therapy, and I knew how crazy she was about Brad. I didn't know yet what was going on inside *him*. But after some discussion, it became apparent that his jealousy wasn't really about Teresa; it was about his own fear of loss. Because Brad didn't feel good about himself, he projected his insecurity onto the stranger in the restaurant. He felt that Teresa was so wonderful and he was so inadequate that any man could easily steal her away from him. His personal issue had found its way out of his inner world and into his—and Teresa's—present experience.

As we talked, Brad began to see for himself that his jealousy and fear were related more to his own insecurities than to Teresa's presumed roving eye. At first he was afraid to admit that his envy, low self-esteem, and abandonment terror were affecting what he thought he saw in the restaurant. Brad's inner conflicts were complex, and it took some time for him to understand how his relationship with his rejecting and critical mother had created a wound inside him that he was now projecting onto his current experience. He had felt disconnected from his family, especially his mother, who had frequently rejected him when he wasn't behaving the way she wanted. Many years later, with a different kind of love at stake, he was haunted by those same feelings. He was reliving his experience with his mother, except it was in the present.

Projection works just like it sounds. We project something that is inside us—a feeling of powerlessness, weakness, inadequacy, or fear—onto a present experience without even knowing it. What we project onto others often comes from painful early experiences that still live in our unconscious. When experiences are too painful for an infant or child to cope with, they can be split off from awareness, held in a safe place where the conscious mind need not confront them. But the feelings they create, not having been processed properly, are fragmented, loose, and chaotic. They take on a life of their own, and when an experience in the present stimulates them, they can burst forth in a dramatic display. The pain that is thus projected seems very real to the person experiencing it. So if we're unaware of our internal process, we are at the mercy of our own inner turmoil, and so is the partner onto whom we're projecting our anger, shame, or fear. Of course, it's not just childhood pain that affects our present conflicts, but all pain, no matter when or where in life it's experienced. The same is true for healing relationships. At any point in our lives we can be affected by love and kindness, whether in an intimate relationship or from a trusted friend, counselor, or spiritual advisor.

The difference between childhood pain and adult pain is that we are usually conscious of adult pain, which makes it less likely to erupt unexpectedly. Childhood pain, as we have discussed, is spirited away from consciousness because children cannot process it; they are not mature enough to know what it means or how to react. So the mind does the child a favor and stashes it in the unconscious. The only problem with this is that the stored pain has a life of its own—it can come streaming out at a moment's notice when stimulated in adult life, and it can be quite powerful and damaging, without our knowing what it really means. However, when we can see what it is we are feeling and understand where it is coming from, we can make decisions about what we want to do in response to the current situation that is stimulating our old pain. Once the unprocessed internal material can be identified and understood, we have some control over the outcome.

Brad eventually understood that he was afraid Teresa would throw him away just as his mother and other women in his past had done. Just like a beach ball held under water, his repressed anger had popped up that day in the restaurant. When his wound spoke, it said to him, *You are insignificant compared to that handsome man over there.* The residue of early rejection, his resultant self-esteem conflict, and his fear of loss had a powerful effect on Brad's perception. In that moment, reality shifted: Teresa's casual look around the restaurant was no longer innocent, it was another rejection. But once Brad could see how the pain of this wound, long hidden, was being projected onto Teresa, he could release his jealousy. He learned something important about himself, and this awareness led to a better understanding of who Teresa was, which helped him differentiate between her and his fear. They worked through the conflict together, and they're now married.

Our Funhouse Mirror

Many conflicts, like Brad and Teresa's, arise out of internal distortions caused by early painful experiences that have morphed into who we believe ourselves to be. Like reflections in a funhouse mirror, these negative images are not true. When children feel neglected, they come to see themselves as unimportant; this feeling then determines behavior in and around love relationships. We may feel these inner falsifications as self-esteem or shame issues such as feeling unlovable, bad, ugly, inadequate, or weak. The distorted sense of a personal deficit is projected right into most couple conflicts, often unknown to the person doing it.

Recently, Brenden came in for therapy with Mary, his wife of many years. We were talking about his father, for whom he had many times expressed loathing. This time, Mary was the one being critical of Brenden's father, and he was defending him. I mentioned that he was being particularly positive about his father and noted that I had not seen this in previous conversations. He took offense at my neutral comment, as if I were telling him that there was something wrong with him, and suddenly got very angry at his wife and at me. To get to the source of the trouble, I asked Brenden if he felt that I was diminishing him in some way, and he snapped back, "Yes, you are!"

As we began to unravel his distortion, we discovered that he felt inferior to both his wife and me, so when I expressed an insight, he thought I was demeaning him. He realized that his feelings of inferiority distorted his perception so that even an innocuous comment sounded like a put-down. He could see that he had behaved that way many times with his wife. He realized that the people he thought were making him feel bad about himself were the same people who loved and cared about him. When he found that it was his own sense of deficiency that he was responding to—and that not only were we not putting him down, we were supporting him—he calmed down.

Grasping how our inner life affects our relationships is challenging. We defend against having our inadequacies exposed and then feeling humiliated, and our defenses come into place automatically, without our conscious effort. Our mind and body interact with each other in intricate rhythms of which we are often not aware. The complex interaction between our temperament, our experiences with family members or lack thereof, and the life we have lived—and the sense of self that arises from all this—is difficult to grasp. One thing is clear, though: our personal pain is a message from our past, and if we know what it is saying, it does not have to disrupt our ability to love. In this sense it's never too late to know ourselves better. Self-knowledge is the road to self-acceptance, offering true transcendence of our painful past. In this way we invent a new way to love someone, even when he or she has behaved badly.

THE DEFENSE MECHANISM

The distortions we've been looking at are all powerful defenses—our psyche's automatic response to the possibility of being hurt. Defenses are built over time to shield us from the effects of painful experiences, specific defenses for specific kinds of pain: a powerful defense against feeling inadequate, for example, is an attitude of arrogance and entitlement. This is how our sense of reality is shaped by our inner world.

Conflict evokes our entire life experience, especially in close relationships. Our self-image is molded from our experience with people we have loved, and it shapes how we respond to the world of others. If our identity was largely formed by tragedy, pain, loneliness, or violence, this emotional information will adversely affect our sense of reality, our ability to love, and the way we relate to our partner.

What Saved You Then May Be Killing You Now

Children learn coping skills so they can manage their inevitable struggles with family and peers. But the very same skills that helped them to survive emotionally as children may hinder their ability to maintain intimate bonds as adults. If our major coping strategy was to tune out family conflict, this same behavior may create fresh conflict in a current relationship. If our family style involved screaming and yelling at each other to help stave off pain, and we do the same thing with our mate, it will break our emotional connection. If our parents were tyrannical and critical, we will tend to act the same way toward our loved ones. If we were punished for having needs as children, then we will have difficulty expressing them now.

A major cause of unhealthy couple conflict is the inability to understand or articulate feelings and needs. The learned habit of blocking emotion creates distance between partners, which in turn causes resentment and withdrawal into anger, along with a host of negative thoughts and behaviors both within and between partners. Left unchecked, this dysfunctional process can drive a wedge into a relationship. When the expression and discussion of needs and feelings plays an important role in daily conversation, many disputes and breaks in our connection can be avoided. But how are we to do this if we don't accept that we are allowed to have needs, or know what our feelings are telling us, or even know how to express them?

The Mind Trick

Let us consider the case of Dennis and his wife, Sharon. Dennis felt inferior and feared that Sharon would leave him if she discovered how inadequate he was. But he wasn't aware of this on any conscious level. Instead, he treated Sharon as if *she* were vastly inferior. He came at her with contemptuous verbal onslaughts, criticizing her for being overweight and selfish, but when he imagined that she was criticizing him, he reacted with defensive aggression and humiliating language: "You're nicer to our dog than you are to me."

For her part, Sharon didn't understand what she was doing to deserve Dennis's contempt. Confused and hurting, she became sullen and petulant. She went shopping and overspent. She ate too much. All of these behaviors only served to make Dennis devalue her even more.

What was really happening here? Dennis's defenses had shifted his reality as he angrily defended himself and devalued Sharon. He didn't see that his need to devalue his wife came from his fear of needing her so much. But together we delved into his fears, and he was shocked when he realized that his devaluation and anger were the by-products of his own terror of humiliation through the exposure of his inadequacy and the abandonment that would follow. Unconsciously, his criticism was intended to weaken her so she would be too fragile to leave him.

After a considerable amount of work, Dennis understood that he was expressing his fear of abandonment through his defenses. He had reconfigured reality in such a way that *his wife* was the inadequate one, not he. What astonishing trickery! His mind made the shift to give him safety from the horror of once again feeling all alone in the world, all in the service of self-protection. It was tough for Dennis to acknowledge that he felt so negative toward himself, but he did it because underneath it all he could not imagine life without Sharon.

Breaking Through Our Barriers

Acclaimed writer and child-abuse expert Alice Miller writes in *The Drama of the Gifted Child,* "Whatever we push out of our own garden we find in the garden of our children." We could likewise say that *whatever we push out of our own garden winds up in the garden of our relationship.* Clearly, understanding our shame and its defenses can be critical to our ability to resolve conflicts and create lasting love.

Defenses that arise out of old, deep personal wounds are complex and tenacious; they are very difficult to change. The solution is to build a system *around* our defenses so that we know how to neutralize them when they kick in. This is why it's so important to understand how they work. Because these early processes are not a part of our conscious mind, we need to build positive self-talk to counteract the negative self-messages. As we learn to recognize these negative thoughts and feelings and what they mean, we can learn not only how to keep from acting on them, but how to change them. It takes some focused attention, but it can be done. These messages can be either mental messages, like a critical voice in our head, or emotional, like sinking feelings. The first step is to determine where they came from so we don't blame ourselves for feeling and thinking the way we do. The next step is to identify what the negative messages mean. Now we are ready to counteract the negative messages with what is true. To do this, we need to know what is true, and we often need someone else to help us with this part. Once we know the truth, then we can establish it whenever we need to as a method of changing our inner language to fit reality.

Once Dennis recognized that his attitude toward Sharon was a defense raised against his fear, he could finally tell the truth—to himself and to her: "I feel like you would run away from me as fast as you could if you knew how much I really need you. So I try to make you feel inadequate so that you will stay with me and I can feel like I'm important. I'm so sorry that I've hurt you, but I'm trying with everything I have to hold on to you. It's just not a positive way to keep you. Please forgive me." This statement turned Sharon toward him instead of away, and as she reached out to him they turned a destructive process into a way of creating a deeper love.

GETTING TO THE SOURCE

We've looked at some of the ways conflict in relationships can arise, and we'll shortly explore some strategies for resolving conflicts in a positive way and using the valuable information they give us. But first, let's look a little more closely at the contents of these conflicts.

Layers of Meaning

As we've seen, many couples miss the true significance of their conflicts. Not long ago, I hit on a deeper layer of meaning almost by mistake. While working with a patient, I made what I thought was an innocent comment, but she later phoned me to say that I had been insensitive. I recalled that her husband frequently complained about having to "walk on eggshells" because she was so easily hurt. He reported that when he did speak his mind, she wouldn't listen, but would get angry instead, then require him to soothe her hurt feelings, a rather long and arduous process. His need for her acceptance made him quite anxious to regain her approval when she was angry, so he would apologize profusely. In this way, conflict served as a mechanism to get him to comfort her. But the cycle tended to wear on him, so he began keeping his distance to avoid setting it off. She, meanwhile, lamented their alienation but could not connect the dots. She didn't understand why he had turned away from her.

I brought this up in our next session together. After a careful examination of her experience with me, my patient saw how her need for comfort was being expressed through a conflict style. She could see for the first time how she denied her need for affection and attention only to seek them through conflict and the subsequent soothing she'd receive. When she could see that her conflict with me was her way of expressing her need for comfort in the same way as she did with her husband, she was surprised. She then worked out a way to ask for what she needed, and he was more than happy to give her reassurance when she asked for it.

As I mentioned at the start of this chapter, conflict is multi-dimensional. On one level we may be angry about something obvious, while on another level we are hurting about something less clear and often not known or immediately understood. How do we address the dimensions of emotional content during and after a fight? The first level, or *manifest* content, is what's immediately apparent, what we see on the surface—like arguing about a comment or who forgot an anniversary. We can refer to the deeper levels of meaning within our psyche as *latent* content that emanates from painful experiences: for example, someone in our lives was critical of us or we feel our mate is telling us that we are not good enough. Taking the time and patience to look for latent content is the best way to work through the deeper and less obvious aspects of our conflicts. When we find ourselves caught in a negative pattern, we can take some time to look deeper to see if there is something down in there that is causing the conflict to cycle around and around.

Into the Depths

We've already seen that our conflicts can arise from pain we suppressed when we were too young even to register it. So how can we tell what is really going on beneath the surface of an argument that reopens our oldest wounds, reawakening infantile longings and furies that are out of our conscious mind's reach? How do we shine a light into *that* dark place? It takes a conscious effort to feel our way into the latent content. This is why it is so valuable to know who we are and what has affected us throughout our lives.

Pop psychologists tell us that simply being truthful is the answer, that "telling it like it is" will solve our problems. With all due respect, "telling it like it is" won't scratch the surface of an intense power struggle that arises from deep shame or from the effects of childhood neglect. Actions and behaviors such as control, rage, contempt, needing to be right, and hurling invectives at one's mate are more often than not related to profound internal issues. The problem with self-help is that it's only a piece of the truth, not the whole truth. Many people with more weighty issues feel stymied and defeated with simple solutions. Most of us are not simple. We are complex, and unless we take those complexities into account, we may not get to the core of our issues. This means we may be doomed to repeat the same negative cycle. What can we do about this?

First, we need to take some time to know what shaped us, what events in our lives made us who we are. Then we need to see how these very same issues, responses to our original environment, are coming up in our current relationships too. If we had our heart broken, we may not want to be close. If we never saw anyone in our family being affectionate, we may create conflict to push our partner away because we don't know how to love him or her. If we were hurt, criticized, and rejected often enough, or we never saw anyone working out problems in front of us, we will be more defensive and unable to resolve conflicts amicably. We can start to dig deeper by asking some basic questions.

- **What is my partner really saying?** Take time to listen to what your partner is trying to tell you. Then repeat back your understanding of what that is. See if you can identify the latent content of your conflict.

- **What does this particular conflict mean to me?** Are you trying to prove something? Are you trying to prove that you are right?

- **Is this conflict about something current or does it remind me of my past?** If this conflict is one that you have had time and time again, then you need to take a step back and find out what you are doing and why.

- **What is really going on within me?** Conflict resolution involves creating a conversation not only with your partner but with yourself. Self-reflection is critical to resolution, because you have to know what you are bringing to the table—what your part of the problem is. Creating a conversation that involves your inner dialogue, what you really feel, takes some reflection. Think about what you are feeling and then think about how you can express that to your partner.

- **What kinds of changes can I make to help my partner understand that I'm trying to do the things that are important to him or her?** Being perfect is not the goal, but making sincere efforts toward doing those things that you have agreed to is the most important aspect of conflict resolution. Agreement without action means nothing.

Particulars and Principles

Defenses that come up during couple conflicts are quite insidious. What appears one way to the person observing a situation may in reality be something quite different. We may think that we are being clear about how we are feeling, when in fact we are really sabotaging intimacy for fear of being hurt. Let us for the sake of this point describe a man who is scared to death to get close because he is afraid of rejection. This fear creates anxiety when he begins to feel close to someone. He might pick fights or do things that he intuitively knows will inflame his partner and push her away. This distance will tend to ease his anxiety, though he won't understand why. Or a woman may not want to make love to her partner because she feels bad about her body. She may start a fight with her mate so she'll have a good reason not to have sex.

When couples cannot agree on what has actually happened in a conflict, it not only adds to the problem, but obscures the issue that may lie under it. Arguing over details leads absolutely nowhere, but couples continue on as if there is a conclusion coming up at any moment. They're really arguing about who is right. It's not going to be resolved; it's circular. I stress that they should stick to the principle, not the particulars of the issue they're discussing. What are they really trying to resolve? The principle of an argument may really be about feeling unloved or uncared for instead of who said what to whom.

Here's a good example: two people are arguing about what movie to see. It gets heated. What is happening here? The discussion of the movie is about the particulars, but the principle may be larger. If one partner feels like the other one doesn't care, then it changes how she sees the selection of the movie. If the other feels powerless and controlled, he will fight harder to get what he wants. The most important point in resolving their argument about the movie is to focus not on the movie but on what is driving the argument. Who wants their way because they don't get it? Who gives the most and then decides that they won't give in? For example, maybe the man feels that if he gives in he will be seen as weak, so picking the movie is how he will demonstrate his strength and bolster his rather tenuous hold on his masculinity. These are principles, not particulars.

So how can we pick the two strands apart? Here are some things to keep in mind.

- Notice what you're arguing about at a surface level. When you find yourself debating who said what and when, you are arguing about the particulars, not the principle.

- Try to understand the real basis for the conflict. What is it that you want or need from each other right now?

- Are you arguing about whether you feel important, valued, respected, and loved? Then talk about that problem so you can reassure each other.

- Make sure you acknowledge each other's point before you make your own.

- Take some time to talk about the kind of relationship you want and what each of you can do to get it.

Conflict at the Confluence

Roger and Louise met when he was in his early 50s and she was in her late 30s. They married quickly, and Louise was soon pregnant. She very much wanted a child and saw this relationship as her last chance at having one.

Roger, who had already raised a family, was utterly unprepared for the prospect of fatherhood again. He traveled so frequently for business that he was unsure he could be available. He expressed fears of aging—would he have the physical endurance to keep up?—and concerns about the idea of raising another child just when his other children were finally grown. He felt, too, that he had failed in his first marriage, and he was afraid of repeating the same experience.

When Roger and Louise first came to my office, they were in crisis. They would recount the minuscule details of who said what to whom, each dead set on being right by placing blame on the other one. They frequently interrupted each other or flew into rages. Roger defended against whatever Louise said to him: "Here I'm working nonstop to support you, and all you do is find fault with everything I do." Louise would withdraw into resentment: "He doesn't see me. He doesn't care about having a family."

Roger didn't like to come home at night because he felt so

inadequate to the emotional demands of family life. Louise was dreadfully disappointed in the man who had seemed to be such a pillar of strength when she first met him. Louise was afraid of relationships, too; she had never had a healthy love relationship before she married Roger. Her father had abandoned the family when she was young, and when her mother remarried, she put her new family first. As a child, Louise had felt invisible and alone. She developed a fierce independence, but deep inside she longed to be cared about and loved. That was part of the reason she wanted a child of her own.

Roger and Louise didn't understand the latent content of their discord. Roger believed that Louise was simply critical, and she thought he was just inconsiderate and emotionally unavailable. They both felt equally aggrieved. Little did they know that their clashes were so connected to their latent issues. But as I worked with them, it became clear that they were casualties of their histories, suffering from the pain that arose at the place where their respective wounds overlapped—the *confluence of pain* that we explored in chapter 2.

It took quite a bit of work for Roger and Louise to understand the true source of their conflict. She wanted him to nurture and care for her but could not express it. Instead, she raged, and he shut down. The key for him was to recognize that his bad feelings about himself were causing him to shut down whenever Louise expressed disappointment. His shutting down was a defense against feelings of inadequacy that were based on his relationship with his father. His defense was to be grandiose and superior, while his deeper self actually felt little and inferior. His self-protective mind needed to hide that feeling from Louise for fear that she would leave him if she knew what he secretly believed. Understanding how this latent content was affecting him and what he was doing to protect himself allowed him to listen better to her complaints. Once he could understand what she wanted, he was more able to respond. She was also able to express her needs in a more positive way.

Roger and Louise eventually realized that in order to resolve conflicts, they needed to determine the true source of their personal problems and hear each other out. The best condition for working their conflicts through positively was to establish a nurturing environment, one that allowed for dialogue instead of argument.

RESOLUTION AND SOLUTION

Interestingly enough, beneath the argument—beneath all our anger and criticism and defending—the message is almost always positive: we want to connect with the person we love. We just can't get out of our own way long enough to express our need for love and care. It's so often the case that just under the surface of an angry adult is a hurt child who deeply longs to be seen and heard but only knows how to scream.

But we can change the conversation if we're willing to do the work. The way our partner reacts to us is a direct result of the way we express our feelings. We can learn to approach conflict in a spirit of cooperation and compassion—and we can learn to avoid the approaches that may be doing us harm. All behavior has meaning; we may not know what it is right away, but it can be known if we take some time to find out.

Some Dos and Don'ts

In his book *The Seven Principles for Making Marriage Work,* John Gottman identifies four destructive styles of conflict—what he calls the Four Horsemen (as in Apocalypse)—that can keep couples locked in a cycle of negativity. As you read the list below, ask yourself if you're using any of these styles when you talk to your mate:

- **Criticism** is often a defense against the fear of being worth less than our partner or the shame related to having needs or depending on someone; it can also arise from the inability to express our intimacy fears, hurt feelings, or powerlessness. Criticism is an ineffective way to communicate and almost always causes defensiveness and anger in response. The best way to communicate our negative feelings is in the form of a complaint, which is different from a criticism. A complaint is about something we want to change; or it's an expression of needs and wants. A criticism is meant to injure the other person, either because we feel hurt by him or her or as a response to our own inner self-criticism.

- **Contempt** is a reaction to feeling ignored, uncared for, disrespected, or unloved. It is about feeling in some way humiliated or about some form of betrayal. Contempt often flows into the void created when we lose respect and trust through what we see as our partner's bad behavior. Contempt is a sign of a very deep split in the emotional connection, and it is very difficult to heal once it arises. Whenever I see contempt, I see it as a sign that the relationship is in deep trouble.

- **Defensiveness** is usually about not wanting to be found out as less than perfect. It's related to our need to feel right, respected, or in control. It's an automatic response to feeling criticized.

- **Stonewalling** is often what we resort to when we can't get through to our partner. It's also a form of punishment, control, or manipulation. Sometimes it can arise from feeling completely overwhelmed, from the inability to form our thoughts or the reluctance to express our feelings for fear they will be criticized. It's also a way to shut out the pain of taking responsibility for our own part in a current conflict.

Beyond fending off the Four Horsemen, couples need to keep in mind some basic concepts that will help them work through disagreements in a positive way:

- **Develop effective listening skills.** Remember to reflect back what you are hearing by nodding, saying, "Yes, I understand," or talking about what you believe your partner means.

- **Practice tolerance.** Learning how to see what your partner is seeing is a skill that is developed by doing. Tolerance is important here because it takes time to fully grasp why we do what we do. Tolerating our partner's behavior while we are learning about what is causing it and what it means is a very important skill in conflict resolution.

- **Tune in to your partner.** Learn to pick up on the messages (verbal and nonverbal) your partner is sending, and then respond with empathy. Tuning in to body language, behavior, and emotional responses is hard to do, but helpful in knowing who your partner is. These skills can be practiced and discussed as you move along together. Sometimes therapy can help.

So how can you cultivate these skills in your own relationship? To start with, work on processing conflicts with understanding, compassion, and support.

In any conflict, it's most important to understand what we are thinking and feeling. What is making us angry: is it that we feel hurt, sad, guilty, or ashamed? Then we need to do the same for our partner: what is he or she thinking and feeling? In practice, this may mean two people sitting down, once they have calmed down, and talking about their experience both within themselves and with each other:

She: "When you told me that you thought I was being silly, it made me feel like you didn't respect me."

He: "It's not that I don't respect you, but that I was trying to tell you something serious and you were making light of it."

She: "Oh, I see—you wanted to tell me about how you were feeling and I made a joke out of it, so you told me I was acting silly, which I was. I thought it might put you at ease to make a joke of it, but underneath I think I was scared that you were looking to me for answers that I didn't have."

He: "All I wanted you to do was to listen to me."

She: "I understand."

Second only to understanding, compassion is a way for us to let our partner know that we feel for his or her struggle. Compassion is the way we connect: "I can see that you are upset; what can I do to help you?" It's also the way we let our partner know that we get what he or she is experiencing: "You seem to be sad that I was not able to be there for you when you needed me most."

Support is equally essential. It means a great deal to us to be supported in the things that are especially important to us, such as our work, an interest, or a passion. Support comes in many colors—it may address one's ideas, feelings, immediate concerns, or deep beliefs. To feel supported in all those areas makes for good connections: "I want you to know that if you feel strongly about building your dream house, then we have to make plans for that to happen."

You can also make other deliberate changes in the way you relate and communicate. When you have a complaint or a request you want to get across to your partner, try softening your message at the start: "I want to tell you something about what I see you doing, but I don't want you to take it personally or feel like I'm criticizing you. When we are with other people, I feel like you get so into the conversation that you forget to include me." Make agreements and take them seriously: when your partner can see that you are actively trying to do the things that are important to him or her, it creates positive feelings. And try to use conflict as an opportunity to demonstrate friendship and practice acceptance. Remember, the way you respond in a conflict will reveal something fundamental about you—either your desire for a deeper intimacy or your automatic defense against the vulnerability of loving and being loved.

The Risky Path

Ivan and Eileen were battle-weary when they first arrived for therapy. Ivan would calmly point to Eileen's imperfections one by one, and Eileen would explode and run screaming from the room. He would then turn to me and say, "You see—she's crazy." Ivan truly believed that his criticism of her was for her own good, that it would make her into a better person. He didn't understand how his criticism was making her stubbornly hold on to her positions rather than change her ways.

Eileen had dreamed since childhood of having a family. She was alienated from her own family and longed for a romantic relationship. She also harbored intense angry feelings toward her father, and they surfaced in her relationship with Ivan. Her father had abandoned the family when she was young and never returned. Her mother had blamed Eileen for driving her father away, and this fostered the rage and shame that she turned on herself and, later, on Ivan. Ivan, meanwhile, was afraid of being abandoned, and he exploited this situation to keep Eileen dependent.

Ivan was every bit Eileen's match in the rage department. He had been a lonely child; his father, a cold and distant man, exerted tyrannical control in his efforts to make Ivan perfect. When Ivan failed, his father would withdraw and not speak to him for days. Justice was meted out with a detached and sinister coldness. Today, Ivan, terrified of intimacy for fear of being humiliated or rejected as he was by his father, meted out a similar justice to Eileen.

Ivan never knew intimacy with his family except through conflict and rejection. So he did to Eileen what he knew, which was to connect through conflict and withdrawal. He crafted unrealistic expectations that she couldn't meet and then, through the resulting conflict, forged a kind of negative, emotionally distant connection. This process made her feel crazy and bad, which in turn made her angry at him. The two of them would argue long into the night about who was wrong and who said what to whom. They would blame each other for causing the problems and then argue about who was more responsible. It was all they knew about how to connect. No matter how hard they tried to work through their rage, they clung to their cycle of blame. Ivan calculated his responses, listing Eileen's inadequacies and failures one by one. Eileen would fume silently, then explode at him in a fury: "You just want to criticize me to feel better about yourself."

Caught in this terrible cycle, Eileen and Ivan could not comprehend how they were poisoning their relationship. But once they understood that their conflict style was actually an attempt to form a bond, albeit through a negative process, they were able to release their guilt and shame about it and thus see more clearly why they kept on concocting irresolvable conflicts. As they peered around the edges of their rage, they began their struggle toward a more positive intimacy. They eventually understood that there was another route, perhaps more emotionally dangerous, but one that would eventually be worth it. They found out that there was no intimacy without risk. As they began the process of opening up, they glimpsed for brief moments how afraid they were to touch each other with their words and how much they feared being thrown away. And as they began to grasp how their relationships with their parents were being acted out in their relationship with each other, they found they could feel great compassion for their mutual suffering.

It took dogged determination to see what had once seemed impossible to comprehend. Ivan and Eileen were willing to look at themselves differently and to include their early experiences in the way they responded to each other. In this way they created the possibility for a more satisfying intimacy. They learned to express their deeper yearnings for love, connection, and approval. They built a vocabulary of emotions and skills that enabled them to articulate what they were feeling and what they wanted from each other without criticism. They began a dialogue about their mutual wants and needs as a way to talk more openly about what made them happy. They developed an ability to discuss openly and calmly what hurt them. They worked on not just blurting out their first thoughts, but taking time to consider what they wanted to say.

How We Treat Others—and Ourselves

When I ask patients if they would treat their best friends the way they treat their mates, they seem surprised by my question. They hadn't thought of it that way. But in fact, the ability to treat our mate as we would a cherished friend is the key to keeping our relationship on track.

We don't always give friendship its due, but it's an important part of healthy conflict resolution. It's also the foundation for creating lasting love. Without it, we can become mired in distrust and insecurity. But if we treat our mate the way we would treat a best friend, we are moving in the right direction. Developing and maintaining a friendship with a good sense of humor and shared interests helps to soothe many small but potentially volatile arguments. When we feel the urge to retaliate, if we can remember that we're with a friend, it can help us to wait a beat and think about what we're going to say before we say it. When we're on the receiving end of criticism or complaints, we can work at being the friend who listens, cares, and wants what's best for the other. If we are being a good friend, then we want to tell our truth in a way that is kind and compassionate, not bitter or harsh. If we treat our partner as a friend, it will help keep us on track when we feel angry and resentful. One important reason why we don't treat our friends badly is that those relationships are less explicitly committed than marriage or romantic partnership, so we run a real risk of losing a friendship if we behave badly. If we add the same value to our relationship, we will be better able to maintain positive feelings.

Of course, this works best when both partners agree on the goal of being friends and then behave accordingly. The true importance of being a friend to our mate is supported by our values about who we want to be in the world of others. What kind of friend, brother, sister, son, daughter, wife, husband, or lover do we want to be? Being a friend is being someone we respect. The gift we give to ourselves is to become someone we admire because we behave in a way that exemplifies our best self. So even if we are alone in the endeavor, the results are worth it because we respect ourselves. We get respect from being respectful; giving and getting do not always go together, but giving is the best condition for receiving.

To resolve conflicts, we must understand that it's more important to be connected than to be right. The Japanese have a term, *wabi sabi*, that means "the perfection of imperfection." Acknowledging, even embracing our imperfections helps us to own up to them when we need to. What I mean by *embrace* is to allow bad feelings about ourselves to come forward so we can consider how we might change the way we experience them. An embrace means that we accept the bad feeling so we can decide how we want to express it.

Knowing what our defenses are defending against helps us choose the best way to express how we feel. For example, needing to be right is often a defense against feeling inadequate or wrong. Being *wrong* means we're bad, stupid, and unlovable. Being *right* means we're good, strong, and therefore lovable. Embracing our need to be right allows us to look deeper. What we see may not be pretty, but it may help us to have a better relationship. The need to always be right alienates our partner, because it means he or she must be wrong, and no one wants to be wrong all the time. And *being right or wrong, good or bad is of no use in resolving conflicts.* What matters most is what's causing the fight and what we can do to make it better. To embrace our pain is to accept ourselves and draw our personal problems near enough to us so we can solve them.

Our failure to accept ourselves can be the source of much contention. Non-acceptance is always projected onto our partner, so our hostility toward our partner for some slight or rejection may actually be a projected image of our own deeply held negative beliefs. Learning how to see more clearly—in part, by listening to what our mate is saying to us about ourselves—helps us determine what's real and what's not. Mastering the ability to see ourselves through our own insight and listening to the responses of others will lead us to a deeper understanding of our true nature.

Self-acceptance is based on the internal sense that we are the product of our experience, not the cause of it. Self-acceptance allows us to take full responsibility for our part of a conflict. We have nothing to prove. No matter who did what to us in our past, it belongs to us now. We are responsible for our well-being, our emotional wounds, and our actions toward our partner.

A New Language of Love

Couples need to learn a language that may be new to them, which is to discuss their differences openly and resolve them positively. This is the language of meaningful dialogue, which allows them to say what they feel and think in a way that is not defensive or critical. If they don't know how not to be defensive, then a defense is sure to come up to protect them from something painful. The goal is for couples to relate in a way that is respectful, thoughtful, and kind, one that will enable them to work through their conflicts more easily and at the same time build a deeper intimacy.

One valuable method for seeing what our defenses are doing—and thereby learning to get around them—is to develop ways to alert each other when they are being stimulated. For example, we might say to our partner, "I understand that what I am saying may make you feel bad, but I am not trying to do that. I am trying to tell you who I am and how what you are doing makes me feel. This is about me, not you." Defenses are most often responses to a perceived threat to our self-esteem, essentially concerned with how we feel about ourselves. The statement above is a way to make a shift away from the personal and so defuse defensiveness. We might also say to our partner, "You are taking this personally and it is not intended that way."

And when it's our *own* defenses that are kicking in, it helps us to remember that when we are defending we are not listening to what our partner is telling us or addressing his or her concerns. We can learn to stop and take in what our partner is saying by acknowledging his or her point first before we say anything about what we think. The essential work of relationships is to build enough trust with each other that we can alert one another when we are being defensive, but also to learn how to be observant about ourselves.

Defusing and Defining Conflict

When you have a disagreement with your partner, there are certain steps you can take to defuse defensiveness and define what's really driving your conflict so you can move on to resolve it. I've arrived at these steps through years of doing couple work, mediation, and psychotherapy, as well as working on my own marriage. After each step, take a moment to acknowledge what your partner has said or vice versa.

- **What is the pain about? (Source of the conflict.)** Where is the pain coming from? Is it about feeling hurt, unloved, or fearful?

- **What are my expectations for my partner that may be unrealistic? (Idealizations.)** Is what you are expecting actually attainable? Can you check that out with your partner?

- **What are realistic expectations for my partner in this conflict? (Reality-based discussion.)** What is it you want from your relationship? What would make it more satisfying? Is that something your partner can reasonably provide?

- **What are my issues, and what are my mate's issues? (Articulating the source of the problem.)** Does the current conflict have something to do with your feelings of self-worth, or is it reminiscent of experiences you've had before?

- **What are possible solutions? (Solution-based discussion.)** State the problem—"I feel bad about never doing enough to please you"—then discuss what you can do together to make it better: "I promise I will try to be there more for you when you are not feeling well."

• **What have we learned from this? (Reflection.)** Maybe you've learned that you need to sit down together on a regular basis and get everything on the table so you can solve your problems before they get too big to handle.

• **Is there a better way to talk to each other to avoid the hurt? (Values.)** Perhaps you can use words that are neutral and make it a point not to criticize, defend, stonewall, or bring up the past.

In the language of love, sometimes the conversation is simpler than we think. A simple thing like letting our partner know that we understand what he is saying by repeating it back in our own words is a powerful instrument for soothing hurt feelings and ending a stalemate. This is an easy way to create connection instead of destroying it. I remember a therapy session in which the husband kept reiterating his point that his wife's anger made him withdraw and he was afraid of her. She kept dodging and defending until finally I turned to her and said, "What he really wants to know is that you hear him." When she stated that she heard him, there was a palpable release of tension. "Thank you," he said. Then we devoted the rest of the session to ways they could work together to create a safe environment for discussion. More often than not, a simple acknowledgement will end an argument altogether, especially if it is tied to a change in behavior on the part of the one who is doing the acknowledging.

Intimacy and Truth

During a couple therapy session, I was listening to a woman who felt lonely in her relationship. I asked her husband if he would turn to her and tell her how he felt. We had worked together for some time, so he was ready for this. He talked about how he was afraid that he would disappoint her and lose her love. She responded by taking his hand and telling him how much she loved him. He was surprised to find out that what she wanted was his truth and the closeness it created. He realized that his myth about being manly, keeping it all inside, and never showing his vulnerability was not working. He was very successful and highly educated, but it did him no good in his emotional world. He needed to open up and so did she. When they were able to express their deepest concerns, it connected them in a powerful way.

Conflict is normal. Resolution is an art. To work through problems and differences with a loving attitude is what creates lasting love. If we take the time to understand the natural complexity of a difficult interchange and then listen to the pleas, the wants, and the dreams of our partner, we're in a place to love more deeply. If conflicts become a source of intimacy, then we are on the right track. This is a wonderful goal to work toward with our life partner. Loving someone in a way that includes both our imperfections will inevitably lead us to a deeply intimate attachment and let us share an ever deeper happiness.

Relationships do not require 24-hour-a-day processing in order to function. Once we learn to soothe the sensitive spots and ease up on our expectations, we're doing what makes love last. Love is made from concern for the other and the willingness to speak our truth openly and with loving kindness while giving our partner the opportunity to do the same. Nothing works all the time, but just being an active participant in our relationship creates a loving place to work out issues that come up in the course of living. This is the path toward an enlightened sense of intimacy—the way we bring light into dark places to discover our true nature alongside the one we love.

For Your Inter-Reflection

How Conflict Can Create Love

1. What are three things you would change about your partner and why?

2. Make a wish list of what you want from your partner.

3. Consider your relationship to both your parents. Can you remember what it was that you argued about? How do the arguments you had with your parents compare to the arguments you have with your partner?

4. Take your latest conflict as a "test case" and try using the steps in this chapter to resolve it. Can you define the problem? Do you know where it is coming from? Can you find ways of improving your behavior?

5. What new responses can you try that will make your partner feel that you have really listened when he or she tells you something's wrong?

cultivating connection

Sometimes our light goes out but is blown into flame by an encounter with another human being. Each of us owes the deepest thanks to those who have rekindled this inner light.

—Albert Schweitzer

"Only connect," wrote E. M. Forster in *Howards End,* "and human love will be seen at its height." In this book so far, we have seen how lasting love depends on a couple's ability to forge and then maintain the precious bond between them. In this chapter, we'll look more closely at ways of creating connection, preserving it through challenging times, and healing breaks when they occur.

One way to think about marriage is to consider the relations between two countries with different cultures, desires, states of mind, wants, and needs. If the countries are to get along, they must use proper protocol, kind greetings, good manners, cordiality, and consideration. From this standpoint, we can think of ourselves as goodwill ambassadors. Being diplomatic when we are expressing a complaint helps make the medicine go down. When we are expressing emotionally charged feelings about what we want and don't want, like or don't like, we are much more likely to be heard and understood if we say it in a way that is respectful and kind.

Considering marriage in terms of two neighboring countries who want to live in peace is a good way to think about what it means to create a loving environment. We have freedom in relationships, but not license to do whatever we want without repercussion or consequence. If we believe that love and respect are things that we earn through our behavior, then we will be much more likely to think about what we say and do. Being civil, diplomatic, and thoughtful goes a long way toward being understood and accepted. The best way to get through to our partner is by being protective of his or her well-being as much as our own.

COMPASSIONATE COMMUNICATION

As we know, relationships do not always run smoothly. There are many factors that influence our thinking, feelings, and attitudes in ways that may conflict with our partner's—among them gender, race, religious background, temperament, sexual desire, stress, career pressures, education level, personal sensitivities, and values. If we take these differences into account in our communication style, we can tailor how we say what we think and feel to our partner. For example, if we know that our partner is biased or has particularly tender feelings about a particular subject, we can take that into consideration in the way we speak to him or her.

Other elements that influence our communication style are the demands associated with things like the cost of living, work, family, friends, personal interests, and health issues. We cannot help but bring these pressures to bear in our relationships. Couples who fashion their communicative style in a way that reflects this complexity create a healthier partnership and ultimately a more loving relationship. This is the goal of healthy couple interaction—to respond to our partner with tenderness and tolerance, amidst feelings of fairness, concern, and a willingness to listen with an open mind and share ideas that include finding common ground.

In the last chapter, we discussed the two levels of emotional content in conflicts with our partner, manifest and latent—both what appears to us when we observe our own and our partner's behavior and what lies below the surface that may be influencing our behavior. Understanding and addressing the latent concerns is often the best way to resolve our differences and difficulties together. For example, if a couple are in conflict because one of them wants to get married and the other doesn't, the manifest content might be a sense of reluctance on the part of one person, but the latent content could very well be fear of failure. If they frame their discussion differently—*What kind of marriage do we want to have and what are we most afraid of?*—they can include in that conversation both manifest and latent content. Bringing the latent content into our communications helps draw us closer because it allows us access to the entire personality and thus makes it possible to end the conflict. Understanding latent content helps us stay in a position of support to nurture both ourselves and our partner.

All this requires focus and time. With all the pressure we encounter in our daily lives, time for this kind of reflection and discussion can be elusive, so we need to deliberately create opportunities to talk about the dimensions of our concerns. The first step is to understand what our basic concerns are, and the second step is to present them diplomatically. The third step is to find some solutions that might work well for both people. For the couple who were arguing about whether to marry, it might work to set a time and date for a decision, then make an agreement to talk about what kind of marriage they want and work through their fears.

Everyone's Talking, but Is Anyone Listening?

Most couple therapy books, along with media psychologists and various pundits, pay a great deal of attention to the importance of communication. Interestingly, in *The Seven Principles for Making Marriage Work,* John Gottman argues that talking everything out is not always the cure for what ails relationships. He asserts that some couples talk very little and still seem to be happy. We might assume that these easygoing couples have less antagonism and are more compatible than others. More likely, though, they're saving their talking for the really important issues. True intimacy is not possible without communicating feelings, needs, and wants on a regular basis; it's just not always important to discuss normal everyday irritations, because they are not really about anything.

Conversely, there are people who feel they must talk every issue through to the bitter end and yet never seem to accomplish what they're setting out to do. This over-processing can be a source of disaffection in itself. Many men, especially, are uncomfortable with long-drawn-out conversations about the relationship. They are ill equipped to process the anxiety and stress that these kinds of conversations can generate. For men, the experience of over-talking often feels like an attempt at control.

Distinguishing what we must work through with our partner from what we can let go is imperative for a loving relationship over the long haul. Not every negative interaction requires discussion. The important points, such as seriously hurt feelings, the way we treat one another, and the need for respect, are issues worth discussing. A bad mood may simply require some time alone. Similarly, some relationship issues are persistent and rarely ever go away completely; therefore, there is little need to discuss them each time they come up. But if our partner continually does something that is offensive or hurtful, we have to discuss it if we don't want to become resentful. The wisdom lies in knowing "when to hold 'em and when to fold 'em."

Problem-Solving Step by Step

Once you and your partner decide that a problem is worth discussing, how do you go about it in a constructive and compassionate way? Here are some steps you can take to talk a problem through:

- **If you're angry, take time to cool off.** No progress can be made toward resolution when you are feeling angry. Anger is a very complex emotion; it's often a response to feeling hurt, sad, guilty, shamed, or frustrated. Take at least 20 minutes apart to think about what your partner may be feeling and then what it is that you are feeling. You can also take a day and sleep on it. It depends on how angry you are or how complex the process is or how long it may take to understand what is upsetting you—and, more importantly, what may be upsetting your partner. The empathy you need to grasp what your partner may be going through cannot happen when you are angry. It is also important to have an agreement in place whereby both of you know that you will talk at some point. Making that agreement allows each of you take the time you need to find out what's bothering you and to cool off.

- **Fully flush out and determine what the problem is.** Before you can solve a problem, you and your partner must agree about what it is. State the problem clearly to each other until you both understand and agree: "I don't think you really want to marry me, so I get very insecure and hurt. When you see me hurt and angry, you feel like I am just angry and unhappy all the time, so it makes you reluctant to marry me."

- **Tell your partner what you want.** Letting your partner know what you want takes the guesswork out of the relationship. What do you expect from each other? What needs are not getting met and how can that be changed? "I want to get married and I want you to want it too. As long as I know that we have the same goal, then I can relax, and you might feel more comfortable moving forward."

- **Listen to what your partner is saying.** Problem-solving depends on affirming feelings and then finding a solution that works for both people. The key is to listen with empathy and then respond to what's being said by taking action—even if that action is simply acknowledgement. Many problems arise from feeling that we aren't cared about and our opinions don't matter.

- **Put the relationship and commitment first.** Make your relationship and your love for your partner the most important value in any conflict—more important than being right or getting the outcome you want. Coming down on the side of the relationship helps create solution-based communication. If you are not working toward a solution, you are not problem-solving. If you are not using compassion, understanding, respect, and empathy in your solution process, you are off track.

- **Apply the Golden Rule.** This is the bottom line: do unto your mate as you would have him or her do unto you.

Dr. Howard Markman, professor of psychology at the Center for Marital and Family Studies at the University of Denver, conducted a study of more than 20 marriages that lasted 25 years or more. He found that couples who experienced the highest levels of satisfaction were those who had developed joint problem-solving abilities. Dr.

Markman discovered that couples' *differences* were not the all-important indicators of marital success, but rather *how couples handled their differences*. How people go about resolving differences is a predictor of how intimate a couple can be. When we think about how we want to handle those differences it makes sense to be prepared. Are you using what Dr. Markman calls "constructive arguing," or are you merely looking to win? If you want peace, love and harmony, then you must remember to add those elements to your communication style.

When couples see how their defenses work and how each one's fears and insecurities are affecting the other, they will be able to reconstruct their conversation. Insight can be daunting, but persisting in negative exchanges that are actually about old baggage is counterproductive. Developing practical insight keeps our intentions clear and facilitates the resolution of conflicts. This kind of enlightenment broadly means the *acquisition of compassion as an intention*. In that sense, *enlightenment* is moving toward the light of positive thinking so that positive behavior will follow. A knowledge of who our partner is, coupled with our willingness to talk about what's bothering us, will help us to actively create both inner tranquility and a loving environment.

Empathy in Action

Geoff and Darlene had been married for six years when Geoff came home late from working on a Saturday to find Darlene miffed because he'd promised they would spend the day together. Instead of arguing and getting defensive as he would have done when they first came to see me, Geoff begged off talking about it, then went to the gym. In the past he would have tried to make Darlene feel guilty by telling her that she was selfish; he would have felt resentful that she was not more supportive and understanding of the demands his work made on him. But now he realized that this was just his way of protecting himself from inner criticism and guilt for having disappointed his wife. Before, he would turn the argument around and blame her so he didn't have to feel guilty or bad. This time he decided to think it through before he spoke. While he was working out, he began to dialogue with himself, using his own words to help himself out. Eventually he came up with what he thought she could hear without taking it the wrong way.

Empathy was the key to understanding where Darlene was coming from and why she was annoyed. She had been looking forward to being together; she was hurt that Geoff did not make it a priority to come home sooner. As he thought about it, he realized why she was upset. She frequently had to wait for him to come home late at night from work and never complained. Geoff had agreed beforehand that Saturday was their day together. He broke the agreement, and on top of it he ran late. Darlene was frustrated because Geoff overstepped his bounds with her, and he needed to acknowledge it. When he returned home, he apologized for not seeing her position, and the tension broke right away. This was a much different outcome than when they first began therapy.

Geoff's ability to think empathically and take personal responsibility for his part of the problem played a pivotal role in resolving the conflict. He and Darlene used this successful model as a template for future problems.

Responsibility and Consideration

Back in the day when I was a teacher, I discovered that most every classroom conflict could be traced to one of two causes: a lack of consideration or an inability to take responsibility for one's own actions, both internally and externally. What came to me after careful observation was that two basic concepts could cover the whole spectrum of discipline: *Be considerate toward others* and *be responsible for your own stuff.* Later, as a therapist, I applied this to relationship conflicts as well. When either partner was upset, it generally revolved around the feeling that one was not being considerate of the other's feelings or not taking responsibility for the messes he or she had made.

Consideration for others and responsibility for oneself and one's commitments are critical to relationship harmony. If we're good team players and are able to compromise, we're actively creating a more loving relationship. Consideration is all about thoughtfulness, being true to our word, and being someone our partner can count on in time of need. The definition of responsibility is that we are *response-able,* which simply means able to respond to what our mate is asking of us.

The Power of Humor

Humor is the great equalizer. It aids in defusing everyday tensions and can end fights before they start. It is a conduit for happiness to flow through.

A few years back I attended a workshop that John Gottman hosted for therapists. He played a video of a couple whom he described as being in a healthy relationship. The couple were discussing money issues, and the whole time they were using humor as a way of dealing with very sensitive subjects. Their ability to laugh at themselves was a healthy way to work out nagging everyday problems while maintaining a positive feeling between them. Developing our own style of humor within our relationship also tends to grease the wheels of reconciliation after a fight. When we can find the humor in situations, it's like saying, "Nothing is so important that we can't find some humor that makes it feel better." The goal is to make problems short and the enjoyment of each other long.

CONSTRUCTIVE COMPLAINING

In all loving relationships, complaints will arise naturally as part of living closely with another person. If we respond to complaints as if they are unwelcome or intrusive, we're more likely to create problems. Complaints inform us, they tell us what's not working, and inherent in them is the potential to make our relationship run more smoothly.

Complaints are not to be confused with criticism. A complaint sounds something like this: "I know you care about me, but I would appreciate it if once in a while you told me that you do." A criticism might sound more like this: "You're such a jerk! You never say anything nice to me, it's always all about you." Criticism attacks; complaints can open up a discussion about how to make it better. Criticism is often a response to hurt feelings and is intended to hurt back. Complaints express needs and wants. Airing complaints is necessary for relationship health, good communication, and harmony. It clears the decks emotionally so that complaints don't turn into criticism or create distance. And if complaints are expressed with tender loving care, it goes even further to create a loving atmosphere. Criticism just creates more hurt and anger and pushes the other person away.

Complaints can take many forms, from expressing our desire to spend more time with our partner to a request for help or nurturing. People believe differently, or were raised with different values, or have different tastes and aesthetics. They may think differently about how they should spend money or even about how they should live life. These differences are fertile ground for complaints that, if they are not expressed or effectively resolved, can grow into resentments that may eventually lead to real distress or emotional deadness. Resolving complaints, on the other hand, is a catalyst for change.

Criticism vs. Complaint	
"What a jerk you are for leaving me all alone all night long."	"When we go to our friends' house for the party, could you please check in with me instead of going off on your own?"
"Do you care about anything besides yourself and that damn TV?"	"We need to make time to go out on a date instead of just watching TV."
"You never listen, you just talk talk talk."	"Would you take time with me when I am trying to tell you something that's important to me?"
"I would think that once in a while you could be nice to me."	"If you really want to make me happy, bring me flowers."
"Do you have any idea how much you hurt me?"	"Could you please ask me first before you tell your friends about something that is very personal to me?"
"You always just run home to your mommy and tell on me, don't you?"	"I need you to not say things to your parents about us when you are upset with me."
"Do you think about anyone but yourself?"	"I need to know that you will be there for me when I'm sick."
"You are such a complete slob."	"Please try to take care of your messes."
"I'm damned if I do and damned if I don't."	"I need to know when I am doing things right."

What Do We Have to Complain About?

Complaints are often multidimensional and address different facets of our emotional life. The important questions are: *why* do we do what we do, and why do we do it the *way* we do? How does it serve us? Is it possible that the reason we're not listening to our mate is because we're angry, or feel unloved, unimportant, or invisible, or all of the above? Criticism, defenses, anger, and resistance to compromise may be indicative of broader and deeper issues. If we're willing to look into the complexity of our reasons for and responses to complaints, we may learn something new about ourselves and our relationship. What are we getting out of complaining or being complained about? Are we ramping up the process by screaming at our mate so she has to listen to us? Or are we trying to protect ourselves from failing in his eyes, or from being rejected? *The most critical skill for couples is to understand how to manage their natural antagonism toward each other constructively. The more couples can put their negative feelings and thoughts in positive frames, the more they will be protecting their love for each other.* When I mention natural antagonism, I am speaking about normal conflict and disagreement between people who come from different experiences and backgrounds. There are no two people who are alike, so most often couples are in conflict about a host of issues, from how hot or cold it should be in the house to who makes the decisions.

In a letter to his brother, the poet John Keats used the term "negative capability" to describe the ability to live at ease with uncertainty and doubt. For our purposes, we could think of it as a coping skill that enables us to manage the negative aspects of life. Couples often fantasize that love is easy and that one should be happy. Then when conflict arises, we want a crutch to hold us up and there isn't one. Instead of yearning for this idealized life, which ultimately brings disappointment, we need to accept that difficulty and differences are a part of life but that this doesn't mean we can't be happy with each other. In this way we develop a sense of reality, hope for the future, and resilience to the difficulties of life without blaming either our partner or ourselves.

From Complaint to Connection

"We don't have a marriage," Allen said flatly. It was clear that he felt frustrated. He complained that Fern was always too tired for sex. He wanted her to be there for him like she was when they were dating, but things were different now: early in their marriage, Fern had become pregnant, and soon afterward she'd gone back to school to finish her bachelor's degree. Allen was afraid that if he told her how hurt and rejected he really felt, she would call him a baby. If he revealed the real source of his complaints, he might hear that she didn't care about what was important to him.

He criticized Fern for being overweight and complained that she didn't cook for him. But at his very core, Allen believed he was unlovable. Although his complaints may have had some merit, he didn't realize how much of his anger was coming from his feeling that he wasn't worth loving.

Meanwhile, Allen's anger and criticism turned Fern off. Her stonewalling caused him to feel even more frustrated, which escalated their conflict. They were at an impasse. After I had several sessions with Allen alone, he began to understand the depth of his concerns and to see that his deepest fears might be unfounded. During our next session he was able to ask for and receive reassurance from Fern. When she found out how he really felt, she was more than willing to tell him that she loved him and would not leave him.

If couples draw on complaints as a resource for understanding each other better and in a deeper way, those very complaints become a way to create a stronger intimacy. When couples are successful at resolving complaints by responding to them with understanding and compassion, they're actively creating security and loving feelings. To understand and acknowledge the validity of a complaint is to be empathic, and empathy is at the heart of all emotional connections. If empathy is a leap of compassion, then to take that leap means that we hear and express complaints in a way that is based on wanting to get through the complaint in the best way possible. The most effective means of expressing complaints is to make them a "we" issue to equalize the responsibility while communicating our complaint—something like "We need to work on making more time for each other." This way of expressing a complaint makes it feel noncritical.

Another couple who came to see me were in conflict over the question of marriage. The woman complained that every time she and her fiancé started to discuss the details, he withdrew emotionally. During our conversation, she realized that he was acting out his fears instead of talking about them. He would arrive late for dinner, be noncommunicative, and forget to follow through on agreements. When she got angry about his inconsiderate and disrespectful behavior, he would get defensive, justify his actions, and stomp out or hang up on her. Then he would pull away, citing her anger as the cause. Because she had felt abandoned as a child, his passivity and withdrawal stimulated her outrage. He, meanwhile, was afraid of losing his freedom and of being trapped in a relationship that he couldn't get out of. These two didn't have a clue as to what they were doing any more than Allen and Fern did.

Both couples had lots of complaints about each other, but they needed to see that their behavior was a way of *acting out* their fears instead of addressing them. When couples express complaints without anger, but discuss what they want and need from each other, they fare much better. But personal pain trumps logic every time. When people feel wounded, especially in the same ways they were wounded as children, and it stimulates their worst fears about themselves, they become angry and want to punish or flee or both.

When Allen acted out his fears of intimacy, it stimulated Fern's abandonment terror and her feeling that she wasn't good enough, so she went ballistic. She couldn't stop her rage because it was just too painful. This was the confluence of their pain. And this is the difficulty that relationships present. We need to understand what drives our reactions if we are to have any hope of containing our pain from earlier experiences.

Does Compromise Mean We're Both Unhappy?

To compromise is to find a place where both parties can agree—a mutual comfort zone. When we compromise, we have to be willing to give up *some* of what we want, but not *all* of what we want. When couples are too busy fighting about who's right, or trying to win the argument, or attempting to change the other person, it renders them incapable of compromising.

Once in a couple therapy session, my patient Steve mentioned that he and his wife, Amy, were having difficulty agreeing about when he should come home after being out with his guy friends. He wanted to be with them to decompress from work stress. But Amy became frightened and anxious whenever he was late, because early in their relationship he had gone to a prostitute after one of his nights out. Now she was never sure what her husband was going to do, an uncertainty that was all the more difficult to deal with because her own history was fraught with abandonment issues. Steve, for his part, had been controlled as a child and felt alone much of the time. As a teenager, when he was alone he would fantasize about the perfect woman and sometimes would masturbate to such images in *Playboy* magazine. Over time his fantasy life moved into the world of prostitution. He didn't understand why he was doing this. His behavior was creating an enormous amount of pain for Amy and he knew it. As a consequence, their issues around compromise were much more complex than they appeared on the surface. They needed to look deeper into their history and fears before they could work out any agreement.

We talked about Amy's difficulties with his behavior, which were related to her father's infidelity, and Steve really listened because he did love and care for her. She, too, was able to be more considerate of his issues once she understood that they came from being a lonely child. He worked on meeting his need to decompress in ways that were more positive; for example, he decided to build a workshop where he could make furniture as an alternative to always going out with the guys. Finally, Steve was able to value the importance of his commitment to his marriage, and once he did, he was willing to work through his sexual issues and compromise. He understood and accepted that he had chosen to be married and that it was his responsibility to care for Amy's feelings. She held up her end of the compromise too: she promised him that when he did go out, as long as he kept in touch with her she would not be angry at him for staying out late.

By working out a compromise that acknowledged each other's feelings, they were able to connect on a much deeper level. As they came to understand what they were experiencing, they created a more intimate bond. As they mastered the way to process their disagreements, they created a positive dialogue that went something like this: "You're telling me that you feel terrified when I stay out late and don't call you. I will never do that again." And in response: "I will try to understand your need to decompress as long as I know that you care about how I feel."

The Source of Anxiety and Fear

Anxiety and fear can profoundly affect the way couples communicate. When anxiety and fear are present, they can create tension, which in turn causes antagonism. Anger is more easily stimulated when these emotional conditions are present. When couples recognize that anxiety and fear are causing conflict, they can work together to soothe the tension so it does not erupt into anger.

Michelle Craske, PhD, of the Anxiety Clinic at the University of California–Los Angeles describes anxiety as the "misapprehension of a future event." Anxiety is linked to the feeling of dread that something bad will happen. Anxiety feels like an 800-pound gorilla just rounding the next corner. We are anxious about loss, being hurt, getting sick, dying, abandonment, or doing something wrong. Anxiety is related to negative thoughts about the future, a sense that something bad is going to happen. It can also be related to a memory of something that has happened and will happen again. In this sense, anxiety is not about being in the moment. One of the best methods for treating anxiety without medication is mindfulness meditation, which teaches how to focus on being in the here and now.

When we are anxious, sometimes verbalizing our concerns in an atmosphere of acceptance helps calm us. Often drawing out our negative fantasies and bringing them into a more positive reality can be helpful in easing anxiety. Couples can work their relationship anxieties through by talking about the unreality of the anxiety and then finding the reality together, which can both alleviate anxiety and bring them closer. Not talking about anxiety, on the other hand, may create emotional distance and make anxiety more intense, thereby causing more stress.

One source of difficulty for couples is their inability to respond or know how to work through anxiety together. When anxiety is not treated, it can lead to depression, and depression in a relationship can lead to the loss of intimacy. Couple conflicts are often based on unresolved anxieties about abandonment or loss. Couples may argue incessantly about unrelated issues, unaware of how anxiety and fear are affecting them. As they learn how to alleviate anxiety and allay one another's fears, they will not only be closer to the source of their conflicts, they will be actively exploring possibilities for creating love.

We all witness our world differently. All we really know is our own experience (and even that isn't always so clear). If we take our differences into account and open up about our anxieties, working it out becomes possible. If we take the time to learn from our mate about what's important to him or her and what makes each of us uncomfortable in different situations, we will inevitably become better able to soothe and be soothed. If we have conversations that include our fears, we will feel acknowledged and supported.

Let's look at some good strategies for working through anxiety together.

- **Describing what you're feeling.** "I feel like you are going to leave me." When you are feeling angry, anxious, or fearful, try to move down into what you think might be causing it from a deeper perspective. Think about what need, frustration, hurt, guilt, or fear is being stimulated and triggering your anxiety or defensiveness. Once you describe the feeling, you are better able to make a distinction between your own initial reaction and the more complete reality of what is actually going on in the moment. Consider and describe what you think is happening with your partner too.

- **Creating calmness.** Expressing fears and anxieties not only creates calmness, but can at the same time simplify the problems you're fearing. Calming statements sound something like: "I want you to know that whatever happens we can work it out together. I'm in this for the long haul and I love you." "Whatever it is, we're capable of finding the right solution if we put our heads together." "As long as we have each other we will find our way."

- **Remembering what's important.** Stick to core values and beliefs that help to give you strength during difficult times. Strong values are very effective anxiety-relief systems. The more you are able to nurture each other during times of stress, the better you will be at *calming* stress. Talking about how much you value your relationship can help ease your anxiety.

SEPARATION AND REPARATION

In every relationship, breaks in the emotional connection will occur, either from the alienation caused by our busy lives or from failures of empathy that happen naturally. These lapses are based on emotional disconnects within ourselves or between us and our partner, and they are part and parcel of everyday life. *The important issue is not that we experience them, but how we repair them.*

How we heal emotional disconnects has a lot to do with our ability to tune in to our partner, of course, but also with tuning in to our own emotional promptings. If we never learned how to repair empathic breaks growing up, then we will have difficulty in our present relationship. We use what we know, and if we don't understand what we're doing, then we're likely to blame our partner for it. If our only method for responding to empathic breaks is to punish or withdraw, we may erode our emotional connection. Once we know how and why we disconnect from our mate, we can find out how to reconnect when that happens. This crucial skill can only widen the possibilities for creating an emotional bond.

Anger, criticism, emotional withdrawal and blame are common causes of empathic failure. If we're paying attention, we can feel the break when it happens. Interestingly, anger may also function as a method of holding on emotionally in the midst of a break. Anger and rage are such powerful connections that many couples will unknowingly move toward those states because they don't know another way. While doing couple therapy, I discovered that often they refused to forfeit their anger or rage. No matter what I tried, they seemed to go back to anger. Finally it occurred to me that they needed the anger to maintain their connection. They seemed relieved when I encouraged them to continue to do what they were doing because the pain of isolation was too great. Once they could grasp the intention of their anger, they were free to discover new paradigms for connection based on loving kindness rather than anger and withdrawal.

Making Repairs

Repairing emotional breaks is an essential ingredient in creating love that lasts. Connection is a survival skill, so we are hard-wired for it. For thousands of years we lived in tightly bound tribal clans; in contrast, today's two-parent families can be lonely places. Susan Johnson writes in *The Practice of Emotionally Focused Couple Therapy*, "Couples must move from alienation to emotional engagement, from vigilant defense and self-protection to openness and risk taking, from a passive helplessness in the face of the inexorable dance of the relationship to a sense of being able to actively create that dance, from desperate blaming of the other to a sense of how each partner makes it difficult for the other to be responsive and caring, from a focus on the other's flaws to the discovery of one's own fear and longings, but most of all, from isolation to connectedness." The essence of what Susan Johnson describes here is that we must be willing to risk opening our hearts and expressing our deepest fears and longings in an effort to create a connection with our mate. Otherwise, relationship distance will ultimately claim us.

Repairing broken connections is a way to not only create harmony and intimacy but build a more loving relationship. Resolving complaints that create empathic breaks is the best way to repair the severed emotional bond. When couples learn to express complaints without criticism and hear them without becoming defensive, they are actively strengthening their connection—but when the complaints start coming, it's difficult to change a lifetime of emotional reactive patterns and then see clearly what our personal responsibilities are. It takes time and patience to create new pathways for emotional connection. Talking about what's hurting us, understanding from our partner's point of view what is hurting him or her, writing a letter, keeping a journal, or simply making time to discuss whatever it is that needs attention—all these are good practical skills in the reparation process.

A broken connection offers an opportunity to strengthen our love—but only if we go about the work of rebuilding with care and skill. Ask yourself if the techniques you are using are the ones most likely to yield good results. Do you have a good understanding of your partner's feelings? Do you need to apologize? Have you acknowledged what your partner is saying even if you don't agree? There are some styles of interacting that will only lead you deeper into conflict and farther away from each other. Avoid these:

- **Turning the argument around.** A very common defense is to turn the argument back onto the other person: "You do that too." This is an unproductive communication style that you and your partner should point out to each other so the conversation can continue about what each of you is feeling and what needs attention within the relationship.

- **Hitting below the belt.** Even though it's tempting to retaliate by hitting someone where you know it hurts, it should be avoided at all costs. There are words that, once said, can never be taken back, forgotten, or repaired. Like crystal, once broken, you may try to repair trust, but the cracks you create will remain. If your mate confides in you about an experience that is very sensitive and you bring it up in an argument to use against him, you are hitting below the belt.

- **Denial**. Denying that you did anything to hurt the other person creates more conflict and contempt. If your partner is telling you that you hurt her, chances are you did something to upset her. To deny it only adds fuel to the fire. The best solution is to stop and validate her feelings first: "I see that I did something to offend you. I'm sorry; I did not intend to harm you."

- **Bringing up the past**. Another dysfunctional move is to bring up a list of injustices that you have saved up to dump out on the other person during an argument. These injustices serve as a distraction from the actual source of the anger (what you did to make her angry) and are meant to direct the blame back onto your partner.

- **Setting fires**. Some people set fires to distract from the real issue. For example, if your mate brings up your stinginess during a discussion about his overspending, this is setting a fire to distract from the original subject. Breaking down into hysteria, storming out, slamming doors, hitting walls, drinking excessively, screaming, or bringing up some other problem during a discussion about something else—all these are deliberate distractions.

- **Denying the truth**. There are those of us who will lie to save their own skin in an argument. At the bottom of all this is the fear of feeling bad about oneself or defending against loss. But lying in an argument only makes it worse. If the lie comes out, then trust is shattered, and not only is there another problem on top of the one that is already there, but it may be even more difficult to resolve.

- **Bringing others into an argument**. "Even your mother thinks I'm right." When your partner feels that you won't listen and she gets frustrated enough, she will bring others into the fray as a desperate attempt to get through. If you want it to stop, then start listening and see what happens next.

It's important that you make agreements not to do any of the above. Keep your discussions in the here and now, focused on what you want and need. Make specific agreements about what behaviors you are going to eliminate to resolve the source of the conflict.

Resolution

Emotionally healthy couples are much more able to work through difficulties by letting things slide. They generally have a good sense of humor and can be more positive with each other. The responsibility for good connections lies with both partners. We all wish that someone could take our pain away or give us a magic potion to make our problems disappear. There is no secret potion, but if there were one, it would be our willingness to look at, listen to, and understand what our partner is trying to tell us, and then to try to affirm what we've heard and respond accordingly. If we function well in our relationship, it will be because we're willing to reflect and learn about ourselves from the way we interact with our mate. To create a dialogue whose goal is to shine a light into our mate's heart and soul and our own—this is the basic activity of creating intimacy. If we make an effort to resolve our relationship discord by knowing more about what is causing it, we will be actively working through our own issues as well. And letting our partner know that we deeply understand and accept his or her dark places is a very powerful instrument in the loving process.

After we have ended a fight and know more about what the problem is and what the relationship goals are, it's time to make a resolution statement. For example, "I promise to listen and do something about being more attentive if you will help me by understanding when I have to work late." This statement is a way to voice and agree upon each person's ideas and concerns. It's a good way to keep the agreements in place to avoid the same problems in the future.

The important point here is to keep our word and do what we say we will do. If our partner can see that we're trying to do those things we have promised, he or she will feel touched and will feel more positive and loving. If both people can see that each one is making an effort to do the things that they have agreed to, they will enjoy longer periods of harmony. Remember, though, it's much easier to *know* what to do than to *do* it. Old habits die a long and slow death.

Harmony is more than the absence of conflict. There are positive ways to build connection too. Try some of these:

- **Teamwork.** If you see a full wastebasket, it won't kill you to empty it. If you take off your clothes, it only takes a minute to hang them up. If you see that your mate is tired and give him a hand, he will love you more for it. These small things can have a large effect on feeling loved and cared about. Other examples of teamwork are: working out a budget that both of you can live with, making improvements that you both feel make your home better, finding a television show that both of you like, or reading together.

- **Love frames.** George Bach was one of the first psychologists to talk about discord in relationships. He offered a means of avoiding conflict and creating more love with a concept called "love frames." Love frames are simply statements about the way we want to be loved and what we do when we are expressing love. For example, "The way I like to be loved is to receive flowers" or "I feel the most loved by you if you rub my back or want to be intimate with me." The other side of the coin is what each person does to show love, such as "Whenever I want to show you how much I love you, I wash your car" or "When I'm feeling especially loving, I want to cook you a great dinner."

- **If you want something, ask!** So often people simply expect the other person to "know" what to do without ever being asked. It's like sex; no one knows exactly what will bring you to orgasm but you. If you don't tell the other person, she may not know. The rule should be that if you cannot ask, you cannot get angry with your mate when you don't get what you want.

- **Acting on agreements.** Whatever you agree to as a result of repairing an emotional break, if you follow through, you will create positive feelings.

Big Expectations, Big Disappointments

Most everyone has a myriad of expectations. We expect good manners, we want people to call us back when we call them, we expect our family to give us presents at holidays and birthdays, or we expect our mate will love us unconditionally. We may expect ourselves to be perfect or expect that our mate will always be strong and be there for us all the time. For perfectionists, expectations are about the right way to behave, such as an expectation that our mate is telepathic and will know what we are thinking. But our expectations can be way out of whack. We may deem that our expectations are simply the way people should live life. We are then quite astounded and angry when our expectations are not met. For example, some people believe that their mates should be romantic and selfless at all times. When this doesn't happen, they think that their lovers have failed them. In a mature relationship this can become a major source of contention.

Here's what expectations may look like:

- *If you really loved me you would make love to me every night.*

- *You should know what I want before I do.*

- *You should always know what to do to make me happy.*

- *If you loved me you would buy me expensive presents.*

Obviously, the downside of expectation is disappointment. Unrealistic expectations are idealized or fantasy versions of real life. Disappointment is our reaction to the difference between our fantasy and reality. When we can't meet these expectations, we feel like a failure. When we attempt to do everything we can to meet our partner's expectations and still can't fulfill them, we stop trying. If, on the other hand, we have realistic expectations, then what our mate actually does is greeted with happy surprise. *The critical point is to know what realistic expectations are.* To find realistic expectations, we need to understand what we want and need from each other. In this way we can learn what we can expect from our relationship and gauge what may be too much or not enough.

Expectations are often built around unmet personal needs. The less able we are to meet our own needs, the more we will expect from others. But this doesn't mean that we must meet all of our own personal needs or that we can't depend on others. For expectations to be realistic, they must be founded in reality. Can my wife give me some of her time right now, or is she too busy? Why do I need my husband to tell me he loves me so often? The more we fantasize about how others "should" be in order to soothe our personal insecurities, the more we will expect of them and the more disappointed we will inevitably feel.

Let's take, for example, the expectation that others should be on time. If we're always on time, then we tend to expect others to do the same. We get angry when others aren't punctual. We feel justified in our anger at our mate or friend. After all, this person was being disrespectful. If we look into the origins of time issues, we see that not everyone was raised the same way. Some households just don't run on time, and the children in those homes may never have learned to be on time. And as we look deeper into ourselves, we may find that our anxiety about lateness is connected to fears of abandonment and insignificance.

Learning that we can manage expectations through understanding and empathy toward others can only have a positive effect on our relationships. Recognizing that we're making others responsible for our anxiety about time helps us to develop more realistic expectations that help us work through our deepest fears. We must ask ourselves what's more important, being right or being happy in our relationship?

The task of working out our anger and anxiety is the key to keeping expectations healthy. If we can't work out our own anxieties, then we will look for others to help us out. If our mate is our only resource for anxiety reduction, we create an expectation that he or she will always be available to help us when we need it. This is not a realistic expectation. No one is that available. It creates a natural state of disappointment and resentment on both sides. We can't afford the fallout from this behavior; it is bound to erode our connection. The resolution is obvious: we need to take care of our own anxiety and relieve our mate from being solely responsible for neutralizing it.

Alienation is unavoidable because no two people can be connected all the time. If we use this knowledge to create realistic expectations, we will not overreact when we experience the inevitable loss of connection. Learning to consciously and thoughtfully create connections based on an intrinsic grasp of what's realistic allows us the freedom to experiment with different and unique relationship ideas. To play and venture into new worlds with each other gives rise to innovation and rebirth, which brings us from distance to intimacy and from anger to joy.

CONNECTION FROM THE INSIDE OUT

Claude Lévi-Strauss, in his seminal work *Tristes Tropiques,* set the tone for social anthropology by studying the indigenous people of São Paulo, Brazil. While trying to understand the nuances of tribal culture, Lévi-Strauss found that he could not apply the classical notions of anthropological research. The culture he was studying didn't fall into any predictable pattern. He discovered that the only way to create an accurate cultural model was to develop the model from the culture itself, not from any preconceived notions about what it should be. He illustrated this point by describing how the tribe members tattooed themselves. When he copied the tattoo on paper, it bore little relation to what it looked like when it was applied to the three-dimensional person. So he classified the people in the culture's own terms rather than trying to fit them into a superimposed structure.

The same is true of relationships. We must derive meaning from the way the relationship *is,* not from the way we think it's supposed to be or the models we have learned from our family. We must construct a new meaning—a relationship model shaped by the needs and wants of each person within a unique relationship.

Making a Vision Statement

A vision statement is one important step in defining our own relationship model. We can think of it as a footpath that we follow in our quest for an evolving, lasting love. A vision statement could be about a value such as enlightenment, harmony, change, new horizons, or peace. We make vision statements because they help us identify what's important. Vision statements can be spiritual, religious, philosophical, or practical. They set the tone for the decisions we make together and the direction we take. Of course, a vision statement is only one way to create a relationship ethic. Other sources of ethical and moral identity include areas of mutual interest, such as volunteering, philanthropy, creative activities, or extended family.

Here are some examples of vision statements:

- **Unfolding love.** We want to create an accepting relationship that becomes a safe place in which to let our love for each other unfold like a rose.

- **Harmony in our relationship.** We want to be always in tune with each other and to work toward deep understanding.

- **Ecstasy as a goal.** We want to create emotional freedom, to love, to laugh, to be ecstatic.

- **Loving kindness in the way we treat each other.** We want to concentrate on being truly kind toward each other in everything we do—not to raise our voices, swear, or call each other names, but to always be kind.

- **Creativity in the way we live.** We want to live a creative life together in which we share our thoughts and feelings in an effort to create new ideas.

- **Tenderness toward each other.** We want to be tender in all things, to support, nurture, and understand each other.

- **Circle of life as our commitment.** We want to be a part of life and live in humility and in connection to all living things.

- **Joyousness as our life goal.** We want to bring joy to our relationship and to our friends and family.

- **Charity toward others and each other.** We want to live life in a charitable way by giving to others and helping those in need.

A Theory of Love and Work

Throughout my years of doing couple therapy, I have observed certain things couples do that really work. As we examine some of the activities successful couples engage in to make their relationships run more smoothly, think about how you might use these techniques in your own relationship to create connection from within.

- **Adjusting and adapting.** We need to accept that some things inevitably change and some things remain the same. Successful couples know this. As we live our lives together, we must allow for change. Feelings evolve, differences emerge, and new ideas and interests arrive. If we make room for these developments and keep up an ongoing dialogue about who we are and who we want to be, then we're involved in a healthy life process of change. Change is not just inevitable, it is helpful for long-term relationships. Relationships *need* to adjust and adapt to remain vital. We simply cannot expect to create excitement and passion within our relationship by always doing things the same way. We must continue to search for new ways to develop our personal happiness and to bring this excitement into our relationship so we can love more intensely.

- **Accommodation.** Accommodation is like adaptation, but whereas adaptation takes place within each of us, accommodation involves the other person. Accommodation is the opposite of constraint, and ultimately it is what makes change possible. When we refuse to make the necessary accommodations for new ideas and interests, love deteriorates. The accommodations partners make for each other's interests, needs, creativity, friends and family, and preferred way of living are very important for long-term compatibility. Live-and-let-live accommodations allow each of us to be who we are without judgment. *When we are free to be ourselves, we can love freely.*

- **Interchange.** Interchange is the process by which couples make time for feedback and problem-solving before small problems become too large to handle. This is necessary for a relationship to function in a harmonious and creative way. Positive, active, ongoing discussion about boundaries, values, and interests makes our relationship function better and keeps our connection vital. Healthy relationships involve interchanges that allow for the communication of a whole host of ideas, concerns, hopes, and dreams. Healthy interchanges include perceptive, descriptive, sensitive, and honest expression of feelings, of what we want and need from each other, without defensiveness, judgment, criticism, or contempt. Healthy interchanges require personal health. We must be free of our own encumbrances to be able to listen with an open mind and heart.

- **Negotiation and compromise.** Negotiation is fundamental to resolving conflict and creating connection. What are we willing to give up, and what is too much? The key is to know when enough compromise is enough. Compromise, as we've seen, means we get what's most important but not all of what we want. Negotiation is the central working process in a relationship because it relates directly to the different ways we see the world and each other. Negotiating is the method we use to find the spot where our views meet and both people feel comfortable. Fairness is the guiding principle.

A Safe Place to Love

It's natural to be afraid to love deeply and to put our heart in someone else's hands. Being able to count on our partner, to feel as if he or she has got our back, is critical to creating a safe place to love. Taking time to work through complaints, getting to know our mate, and understanding what makes him or her hurt or feel loved and cared for is what allows our love to emerge from behind the safe but isolating walls that protect us.

Creating safety in our relationship means:

- Feeling that our partner is looking out for us.

- Knowing where our partner's wounds are and learning how to avoid stimulating them.

- Asking for and receiving comfort when we need it.

- Knowing what makes us feel loved and what we do to express love.

- Feeling valued and respected and helping our partner feel the same.

- Not letting complaints build up.

Are we willing to learn how to live well with others and take the time to find out how our mate truly sees us? How many of us have learned from our mistakes? If we want our partner or our children to love us, what must we do? What we must do is to become the kind of person who deserves to be loved. Getting there is the hard part. If couples do take the time to look at what makes them angry, selfish, mean-spirited, or sad, then they can use that understanding and self-knowledge to connect more directly and deeply with each other. In this sense, the most important relationship we will ever have is with ourselves. The more able we are to be self-accepting, the more we will be accepting. The more able we are to be caring about ourselves, the more caring we will be.

For Your Inter-Reflection

Cultivating Connection

1. Think of a complaint that you often make to your partner. Does it come out sounding like criticism? Can you think of another way to phrase it, without criticizing, to express something you want or need?

2. Take a common complaint you make—the same as above or a different one, such as "No matter what I do, it's never good enough." Does it have anything to do with how you feel about yourself? Are you taking something your partner has said too personally? Perhaps your partner is really trying to tell you what he or she wants or doesn't want. Is this a bad thing?

3. Think about the common defenses we've discussed. What defenses do you use or see your partner use in your conflicts? What are some alternatives?

4. Make a list of your expectations for your partner. Ask your partner to do the same. Then share your lists and discuss them. What do you know about your partner that you didn't know before? What can you change? From each list, cross off the unrealistic expectations, then make a new list of things you can realistically expect.

5. If you were to make a vision statement for your relationship, what would it be? Write down some ideas and ask your partner to do the same. Then compare notes and come up with a vision statement together.

the dynamics of desire

Sex contains all,
Bodies, souls, meanings, proofs, purities, delicacies, results, promulgations,
Songs, commands, health, pride, the maternal mystery, the seminal milk;
All hopes, benefactions, bestowals,
All the passions, loves, beauties, delights of the earth,
All the governments, judges, gods, follow'd persons of the earth,
These are contain'd in sex, as parts of itself, and justifications of itself.

—Walt Whitman

LIKE ALL ADULT PROCESSES, sex is integrated and embedded in couple relations. Sex is a wonderful outlet for the expression of love, and it can be a barometer for the health of the relationship as well. Sexuality, after all, is the most powerful of all human interactions.

In my experience with couples, sex is like a snapshot of the relationship as a whole. Because it's such a powerful experience, it taps into the core of relationship health and connection. For couples who feel close, supported, safe, and loved, sex tends to be a regular and pleasurable activity. When people feel unsafe, unloved, or not secure, sex is usually problematic. Either way, understanding the role it plays in our relationship helps us gain important insight into who we are together. Sex is not necessary for survival, but it can be critical to the survival of our relationship.

SEX IN RELATIONSHIPS

Sexuality is an intense yet fragile emotional system within a relationship. When sex works, it's because couples can open up about what they want, their fantasies, feelings, and fears. When they engage in an erotic dance that involves exploration and playfulness, they are creating sexual excitement and forging a dynamic bond. But anger, contempt, disrespect, fear, distance, and passivity can drain desire and erode the sexual connection. To have an ongoing sexual relationship that is both monogamous and satisfying, couples need to understand what their partners like and then work to provide it.

What Works and What Doesn't

Sex is inhibited when couples make it a battleground for other relationship issues. So couples who come to therapy with *sexual* issues usually need to look deeper into the quality of their connection. Generally, if they're not intimate, it's indicative of a break in their emotional bond. And though there are many factors that can influence sexual dysfunction—stress, drugs, alcohol, performance anxiety, early sexual abuse, rigid religious upbringing, self-esteem issues, physical illness—sexual dysfunction can also be a strong indicator of unresolved personal and relationship conflicts. People who are obsessive-compulsive, rigid, angry, demanding, not empathic, or not tender with their mates will most likely experience sexual difficulty, unless that's what turns them on. Angry, controlling, and sadistic partners may find those same characteristics showing up in their sexual conduct.

Sex works best when couples agree on what they want from their sex life. Sex is different for everyone, so unique and individual that psychologists generally don't use a single standard to assess what's normal. There is no one-size-fits-all when it comes to preference, frequency, or activity. Not everyone craves extremes, so encounters may range from acting out dramatic sex scenes to going through the motions, from highly passionate to sweetly affectionate to perfunctory. There are no hard-and-fast rules. What brings pleasure to a couple can be whatever they want it to be. Curiosity and communication about pleasure creates excitement.

Sexuality is what distinguishes marriage or a romantic relationship from friendship, and this is one reason why it's so important to keep the fires burning. Passion has a tendency to diminish, but it can continue if couples make time for it and clear the path toward it. Couples who seem to have the most active sex lives are those who make it a priority and work together to make it exciting.

Sexual Agendas

Two partners' desire for sex is rarely an exact match. At any given time, one person may want more or less sex than the other. This is natural; the difficulty arises when the one who's interested puts pressure on the one who isn't. Sexual patterns change throughout life and are subject to inevitable shifts in desire for a host of reasons: stress, illness, depression, monthly cycles, the birth of children, and aging, just to name a few. Couples who survive the ups and downs do so because they communicate with each other about their desire.

Sometimes sexual desire doesn't seem to be about the other person at all. It may be based on fantasy, or it may be exploited as a means of control. For example, we may want sex to validate our self-worth, or to influence someone to do what we want, or to vent our anger. Adding these extra components to an encounter can be a "turn-off" if our partner is made to feel like an object in our emotional struggles. When couples are goal-oriented and march straight to orgasm, then, too, sex can cease to be about desire for the other person and instead become desire for the effect that sex has. Or our sexual intention may be to make our partner orgasm because we need to succeed, to possess, or to win approval.

If we detect that sex has become harmful, we must address the problem or risk the possibility that it will interfere more and more seriously with future encounters. Flushing out the rationale for a sexual difficulty, no matter how hard it may be, is the first step. If one person always determines when and where sex will occur, this may prove to be a problem. The general rule is: for sex to be satisfying, couples need to work out a way to balance the desires of both people. Sex works best when both people feel connected emotionally, psychologically, and spiritually. Otherwise, sex may become just mutual masturbation and the ability to create a loving connection may be lost.

Generally speaking, men want to have sex to feel close, while women want to feel close to have sex. Simone de Beauvoir pointed out, in her groundbreaking book *The Second Sex,* that men and women experience sex differently because women are being entered and men are entering. So while the man feels closer once he has entered, the woman needs to feel close *first* in order to allow him to enter her body. In American culture, though it's acceptable for women to show affection toward each other, men are not typically very affectionate with anyone outside their love relationship. Sex is the meeting ground between men's emotions and their desire. For many men, it is the only place where they can express tenderness, affection, and their need for connection.

Sexual problems, not surprisingly, are often related to disrupted connection, unresolved anger, and bitterness. When a woman tells me that she does not want to have sex with her husband or lover, it's typically because she feels a loss of respect for and closeness to him. Of course, this creates further stress within the relationship. If the couple doesn't resolve the issue, a battle may ensue, in which one partner feels misunderstood and the other sexually frustrated—so no one wins.

HOW CAN WE MAKE IT BETTER?

The more couples communicate about their sexual interests and desires, the greater their potential to have satisfying sex. If either partner's inhibitions or attitudes toward sex are causing problems, they need to be discussed and worked through. Affection, humor, sensuality, and fantasy are all good tools to ignite desire and encourage a more satisfying sexual relationship. Two things that can make sex more fulfilling are making space for sex (either figuratively, as in a busy schedule, or literally, as in a home crowded with family) and talking about what turns each person on.

Sex is the most sensitive of human experiences. For this reason, how we talk about sex to our partner is very important for maintaining our sexual connection. How can we tell our partner what we like and don't like without hurting his or her feelings? (For that matter, how can we receive our partner's requests without getting defensive?) Masters and Johnson, in their cutting-edge work *On Sex and Human Loving,* made an important point about this delicate subject when they told us to make "no" sound like "yes." Instead of saying, "Don't put your tongue in my ear," try saying, "I know that you love to put your tongue in my ear, but I get so turned on when you kiss my neck." Making requests, letting our partner know what we like or don't like, is the single most important thing we can do to keep the connection strong.

Getting Specific

Here are some ideas to consider as you and your partner start to talk about your sex life.

You make the limits. You can define sex any way you want it to be. There are no "shoulds" in sex. If something is not working, then you need to find out why or let it go. If you like having sex in exactly the same way every time, then that's fine. The key is to find an approach that works for both of you.

Talk through anxieties and fears. Most often, if we can talk about our fears, we become less fearful. For example, if a man is afraid that he will not sustain an erection, he can talk about it to his partner, and if he feels understood and accepted he will feel less afraid. If he knows that he can do whatever he is comfortable with, he can feel safe.

Do not take anger to bed unless you like it that way. If you find that you are holding back or losing desire, you may actually be angry. If there is tension between you and your partner, you will feel it sexually. Or your past experience with sex may be interfering with the situation of the moment. If you were abused somewhere along the line in your life—or are being abused in your present relationship— that will affect you sexually, too. Anger can be a powerful turn-off. It is helpful to either talk it through or bring it into the sexual act in a way that feels safe for both of you. One of the elements of sexual

Ask Your Partner

- Where and how do you like to be touched?

- What's your best sexual fantasy?

- Are you anxious about any aspect of sex?

- Can you show me how you achieve orgasm?

- Do you feel pressure to achieve orgasm?

- What turns you on?

- What turns you off?

desire is danger, after all, and many couples like to create a sense of danger in a safe way to heighten the experience.

Know your body. For sex to be satisfying, you may need to help your partner help you. For example, a woman may want to express her desire for orgasm by showing her partner how to help her reach it. To learn more, consult *The Hite Report* by Shere Hite, an excellent book on female orgasm. According to Hite, women reach orgasm differently from one another, each in her own special way. To understand that way takes communication and experimentation. The best way to be a good lover is to ask your partner what he or she likes or doesn't like.

Take the pressure off performing. For many men, erectile dysfunction or anxiety about it can get in the way of satisfying sex. A few things to keep in mind:

- Erections are not the only way to experience pleasurable sex.

- It's a myth that you have to respond with an erection whenever a woman wants you.

- It's possible to lose an erection, take a break from sex, then get it back and resume.

- When you're anxious, blood flows to your heart (and away from your penis), so being nervous can *literally* make you lose an erection.

- Finally, there could be a medical reason for dysfunction.

It often helps to shift the focus away from the need to perform. Try talking with your partner about any concerns or fears you have—or take your clothes off and then just hold each other. Affection can be satisfying on its own.

Explore spiritual sex. The interest in spirituality that's growing in American culture has made people aware of a whole variety of spiritual pursuits, including Tantric sex—a disciplined practice that attempts to join sexuality with energy to make it a conduit for a transcendent connection. Margot Anand has written a book titled *The Art of Sexual Ecstasy* as a resource guide for couples wanting to work toward a spiritual sexual connection. She explains:

> When sex is just an unconscious, mechanical urge in you, it's wrong. Remember, sex is not wrong; the mechanicalness of it's wrong. If you can bring some light of intelligence into your sexuality, that light will transform it. It won't be sexuality any more . . . it will be something totally different, so different that you don't have a word for it. In the East we have a word for it, Tantra. In the West you don't have a word for it. When sex becomes joined together, is yoked with intelligence, a totally new energy is created . . . that energy is called Tantra.

Discussing Desire

As important as it is to talk with our partner about what we want our sex life to be, it's just as meaningful to keep communicating when things don't go as we would like. Let's look at one couple who were able to bring their sexual difficulties out into the open and trace them back—like so many relationship challenges—to their roots in their early experiences.

When Harry met Sally they were in their late 40s. Harry had been previously married to his high-school sweetheart, who had become pregnant at 17. In those days it was unacceptable to have an abortion or to have a child out of wedlock, so they married. It was a mismatch from the start, and after many years of trying, they divorced.

Harry grew up in a home that was emotionally distant. His father rarely showed him affection or interest. His mother was dedicated to his father and his younger sister. Harry mystified his parents. He was a dreamer and loved to draw and make things. Eventually he became an architect. He tried all his life to gain his father's approval but never got it.

Sally was raised by nannies and maids because her divorced mother was often away on business. Her father disappeared early in her life and died when she was quite young. Her mother was controlling and strict; Sally could not express anger toward her without serious consequences. Sally was outwardly happy and carefree, but inwardly angry. She became a successful surgeon, but the rigorous demands of her education and training kept her social life from developing normally.

Both Harry and Sally had been single for many years when a friend fixed them up. They were quickly enthralled with each other. Sally saw Harry's artistic nature as the unfulfilled part of herself, and Harry enjoyed how much Sally loved his work. Not long into their relationship, they moved in together.

After about a year, their sex life began to wane. Sally felt a lessening of her desire for Harry, who constantly pressed for sex. Sally responded by withdrawing; Harry became angry and sullen. He reacted to the lack of sex as if Sally were his disapproving father. When Sally tried to talk to him about her lack of interest, he felt rejected and angry. She in turn felt resentful that he wanted sex to boost his self-esteem and not because he desired her. When they arrived at my office, they were both very frustrated. Harry was angry because he felt rejected, and Sally was hurting because she felt controlled.

In my private talks with Harry, a set of insights began to emerge. His low self-esteem contributed greatly to his need for sexual validation. It made him feel wanted. Sex had taken on another meaning. Sally came in by herself, too, and during our session she realized how Harry's demands made her feel. Once she could see that she was experiencing her controlling mother all over again in Harry, she decided to be more generous with Harry's self-esteem needs. She experimented with Harry and tried to be accepting of his desire for sex. She saw that sex could be her gift of love to him.

As Harry grappled with his needs, he understood how much his desire for Sally had to do with his need for validation. He realized that he didn't want to make sex a battleground, because doing so damaged their intimacy. Together, they came to see how much their personal issues were involved in their sex life.

Harry and Sally developed a pattern of intimacy that worked for them. These days, Sally asks Harry about what he wants and when would be a good time for them to have sex. They play with fantasy during the week and have decided that the best time for sex is on the weekend.

Fantasyland

In chapter 3 we talked about the influence of myth and fantasy on the reality of our relationships. Sexual fantasy is similar to yet distinct from other aspects of our fantasy life. Sexual fantasy can specifically relate to actual sexual encounters or can engage other aspects of our personality, like visions of power, pain, or acquisition that are related to the sexual act but not about a specific person.

Sexual fantasies are our own creations: we are the director, writer, lighting tech, and cinematographer in our fantasy life. Fantasies can play a role within a relationship or stay completely separate, be shared with a partner or kept private. They can either enhance a relationship or create distress. They can be positive or negative: a negative fantasy might contain frightening or abusive visions, while a positive fantasy might portray a romantic scene, like making love to our beloved on a moonlit beach somewhere in paradise. They may relate to punishment and submission, or they may be devoted to romance and redemption. Whatever they entail, they inform us about our deepest desires. They contain important information about our inner world.

This leads us to ask, what can we realistically expect from our sexual fantasies? If we think of sexual fantasies as comparable to dreams—which Freud famously termed "the royal road to the unconscious"—they offer a window into the very soul of our desires. By understanding our fantasies, we may be able to uncover what we truly need from others. If we fantasize about submissive or dominant partners, for example, it may be a relief from feeling too responsible or too submissive in our daily lives. Couples who view fantasy this way can use it as a means of learning something about where and with whom their sexual satisfaction really lies. Sexual fantasies, if expressed appropriately, can contribute to the intensity of sexual life.

It is not necessary to act out or even share our fantasies. Sometimes allowing space in our own mind for fantasy is enough to get our thinking oriented toward intimacy so that having sex with a partner can be more intense and satisfying. Fantasies keep sex exciting and interesting for both people. Fantasy can be especially helpful for couples who have been married for many years, as they can use it to stimulate sexual interest. Discussing fantasies openly with our partner can lead the way to greater understanding and connection with each other. The ability to have fun with fantasy is a key element to making the most of our sex life, but fantasies are most valuable when they're used as guideposts and not rules.

John's Secret

John grew up in a home with extremely passive and emotionally fragile parents. He was seldom able to express his intense feelings or anger toward them, and on the rare occasions when he did, they withdrew or fell apart. His repressed anger was so great that, at a very early age, he learned to pacify himself by masturbating using fantasy that contained sadomasochistic images of dominance and submission. He had to "be nice" and passively accommodate his parents to gain acceptance and love—but once he sexualized his anger, he found a perfect outlet. His sadistic impulses toward his parents developed into sexual fantasies in which he could express his aggression and anger in relative safety. His parents had no control over his fantasies, so he began a rich inner sexual life centered on pain.

By the time he reached adulthood he had wholly sexualized his rage toward his parents. When he began to be intimate with women, his sadistic and dominating urges emerged but he was unable to understand where they were coming from. It wasn't that he hated or even disliked women. It was just that his sexuality was tied to his aggression. He couldn't find a way to express himself because he was so ashamed of his sexual interests. Once he married, though, his sexual fantasies came out, and they became a contentious subject in his relationship with his wife, Monica. She liked straight lovemaking and had little interest in BDSM (bondage, dominance, and sadomasochism) or openness to John's urges. They were in conflict about those urges and what they meant for their long-term sex life.

John struggled in therapy to understand and accept his sexual identity. He began to discuss with Monica what he wanted and needed from their sex life, and she asked questions that he was willing to answer. In time, she decided to try and enter his world. In return, he agreed to continue to have straight sex that suited her taste for tenderness. They eventually worked out a way to merge their differences so they both could feel satisfied.

John's sexual tastes will probably not change much, but knowing what his fantasies mean will enable him to discuss them with his wife and use this information to improve their sex life. His understanding about how his aggression became sexual allows him to use this energy in his sex life with Monica but also direct his aggression toward his work and creative interests. He has started doing erotic artwork as another outlet. His insights into the origins of his sexual preferences have freed his wife to share her intimate fantasies too.

WHY MONOGAMY MATTERS

A commercial features a young couple dining *al fresco*. She is pretty and he is handsome. He spies two very cute young women walking past him. He surreptitiously checks them out in the reflection on the screen of his cell phone. His girlfriend is watching this and sends him an admonishing text message with a sly grin, to which he answers, "What?" What this little vignette implies is that men have a roving eye and women have to accept it.

Nonetheless, monogamy is a cultural ideal in Western culture, the standard for straight and gay committed relationships (though it is not practiced in all cultures—plural marriage is found all over the world). During the '60s and '70s, "open marriage" was experimented with, as couples were looking to bring the sexual revolution into the institution of marriage. It failed because the culture of monogamy was too strong. Many couples broke up, and many more gave up the practice.

So how can we reconcile monogamy with our sexually provocative society and our innate appetite for novelty? Is it possible to stay monogamous for a lifetime, especially for those who marry young? Most animals and certainly all primate species, with the exclusion of some *Homo sapiens,* are promiscuous. With this in mind, we will travel this well-worn territory to find some new answers to the age-old question: why monogamy?

Reasons We Cheat

"No adultery is bloodless," says a character in a Natalia Ginzburg novel to a woman with whom he's had an affair. Why, then, do people risk the damage and pain that affairs almost always cause? We watch the news dumbfounded to see one of the most beautiful and accomplished women in the world, distraught and divorcing because her husband cheated with the nanny. We scratch our heads in dismay. Are men hardwired to be promiscuous?

Statistically, men are more likely to be unfaithful than women. There's some reason for this in our evolutionary past. Women tend to be much more monogamy- and family-bound. Men have one eye on the family, but the other one is roving. Some of my male clients have commented about how shallow it is of them to pick a woman whom they find pretty and sexually attractive. I explain that women who appear attractive to them could be expected to create offspring who would have an easier time surviving in a highly competitive society. For thousands of years and across all animal species, the survival of the fittest has ruled. I believe it continues to be a factor in how men choose desirable mates. Men generally depend more on visual cues for their sexual attraction; women are in general more internally focused. That's why we find more men looking at images of attractive partners and more women reading romance novels. We are also the only species that walks erect, so men and women are in effect showing their sex organs, as we see so openly in advertising and fashion media.

Sometimes infidelity arises when there is not enough attraction in the first place. People get together and marry for all kinds of reasons, and they may choose a partner whom they consider a good person even though the sexual attraction is weak. When we choose someone for reasons that don't include sexual attraction as an element of being together, we may lose *all* attraction over time. At this point one or both people may reach out to others for solace. This is not to say that sexual attraction can't grow over time. Even arranged marriages can become romantic. Love can bloom if people treat each other with loving kindness and compassion. But true relationships of convenience can also be lonely and painful and ripe for outside temptations.

Often, though, it's a personal or relationship problem that is being expressed in an affair. A personal issue such as feeling unwanted (because we never felt wanted growing up) could cause a man or woman to act seductive in an effort to transform shameful feelings of being unwanted and powerless into a sense of being desired and thus powerful. There are men who need to conquer women to feel desired and powerful, and there are plenty of women who get a similar charge from conquering—or being sought after by—men. The intensity of a new sexual experience can add excitement for those who feel bored. Not surprisingly, the most common reasons given for infidelity are loneliness, lack of appreciation, and feeling unloved. Love affairs usually involve more talking and commiserating than sex. They begin in a flurry of passion and often end with a multitude of painful imperatives. They rarely evolve into lasting relationships. But in most instances the pain that was created in the initial moral lapse continues in the new relationship. As affairs create new beginnings, the original moral failures can return with a vengeance. When we don't do the work to find out what has caused the original failure, we are doomed to repeat it.

The Girl Can't Help It

Megan and Carlos were high-school sweethearts. She was the popular cheerleader, and he was the cool senior with a car. For Megan, Carlos was the guy from the other side of the tracks, the rebel type that the girls went wild over. For Carlos, Megan was the dream girl every guy wanted on his arm. Soon after graduation, they eloped. Megan wanted out of her house and away from her controlling father and depressed mother. Carlos wanted Megan because he believed her sophistication and family wealth and status would make him whole. What they did not know was that they were going from their respective family frying pans into their own relationship fire. They had almost no understanding of the complex issues that drove them toward each other and inevitable disaster.

Carlos was a "latchkey kid" until his parents arrived home at around 7 p.m. He was the youngest of three children, and after his parents divorced he fell through the cracks. His mother worked two jobs and was always exhausted and frazzled. His father was a meager provider and was frequently unavailable. When he did show up, he bullied and criticized Carlos. As a result, Carlos felt both angry and deeply inadequate. He couldn't express his anger toward his father because he would have been punished for it, so he internalized it, but inside he was boiling.

Megan's unhappy childhood was laced with frequent emotional withdrawals and punishments. She was never allowed to express her anger either. To protect her fragile connection to her parents, she learned to hold her feelings in and be the "little princess" her father wanted. But on the inside Megan was seething with anger. As a teenager, she delighted in sneaking out during the night to have sex with Carlos, knowing that her parents would go crazy if they knew. One of the reasons she selected Carlos as a husband was to make her father angry, to get back at him. But she was unaware of how her anger at her parents made Carlos attractive to her and how this same scenario would play itself out in their marriage.

Carlos fantasized that Megan's love for him would make him feel acceptable. Inevitably, her love was not enough, and he became reactive and critical. He began to treat her like his father had treated him. He defended against his own sense of inadequacy by expecting Megan to be perfect, and when she failed in his eyes, he bullied her, making her do menial tasks over and over. He believed that Megan's main responsibility in life was to take care of him, over and above their children. He thought that it was his right as a man to make all the decisions and be in complete control of her. His inadequacy forged his righteousness, along with a set of rules for her behavior that supported his arrogance.

Carlos blamed the world for his personal failures. He'd been cheated out of his childhood and Megan was going to make up for it. His criticism, power plays, and controlling behavior were the product of his unconscious desire to weaken her so that she would not leave him. He was transforming himself into someone bad and powerful to keep from feeling weak and helpless. Megan, meanwhile, was working her way up as a successful executive in a major corporation, while Carlos couldn't hold a job. His wife's successes made him feel even more inadequate, which drove him to become even more demanding.

After years of suppressing her anger and rage toward Carlos, Megan rebelled. She began having extramarital affairs with his friends and others, and she left a trail a mile wide for him to find. She had no idea of the magnitude of her rage.

Before coming to couple therapy, Megan had seen another therapist, who recommended that she tell Carlos of her affairs to put their relationship on an honest footing. When she confessed her infidelity, his worst suspicions were confirmed. For Carlos, this was a bitter irony. He had married Megan to be loved in a way he had never been loved, and instead it had become a nightmare of rejection and humiliation. He was profoundly wounded by Megan's infidelity, and the pain blew the lid off his smoldering anger. His internal defenses concocted a rage-filled cocktail that transformed him into a righteous victim. From this victim position, he tortured Megan no end. She tried talking to him, but whenever she did, he became furious to the point of violence. "He's angry all the time," she complained in our sessions. "Everything I say starts a fight."

It became clear that Megan was simply enacting the same method of expressing anger that she had as a teenager. She didn't realize at first that her anger toward Carlos drove her to retaliate by having affairs. Once she discovered what she was doing, it was too late; the proverbial cat was out of the bag. Megan and Carlos's marriage broke up because the wounds of betrayal were too deep for him to understand or accept. Not only was his trust broken, but it also confirmed something that he could not acknowledge to himself—that he felt he was inferior as a man. He had to go on the defensive because the confirmation of his inadequacy was too painful to bear. Neither Megan nor Carlos had the emotional resources or self-knowledge to endure the struggle that ensued. Carlos pursued Megan in a relentless and nasty custody battle and eventual divorce.

Ironically, as soon as Megan realized she was acting out her rage through sexual indiscretion, she immediately stopped having affairs and began confronting Carlos with her negative feelings. Had she done that during the marriage, they might have been able to avoid the pain and suffering that followed. Instead, Carlos never did come to any understanding of the connection between his anger and his shame. He remains righteous, arrogant, and bitter, still blaming Megan for his fate in life. Megan, on the other hand, went on to marry again and is now able to confront her new husband with her complaints. She no longer expects things to be perfect.

Megan and Carlos's story brings up an important caution. We often think that trust means total transparency, and indeed telling the truth *is* essential to relationship trust—but it must always be tempered with concern for the feelings of others and the understanding that certain truths will inflict enormous pain. Confessing indiscretions is always painful. We must be sure that this admission serves the purpose of bringing the relationship into a better place, not a personal need to assuage our own guilt or retaliate in anger toward our partner. Sometimes attractions, flirtations, even infidelities are best handled in private, where we can look within ourselves to find the source of the problem and then move on to repair the broken bond.

Keeping Faith

Monogamy is the gift we give to our partner and to ourselves. We feel bad when we behave in opposition to our own values and hurt the ones we love. To feel truly connected, intimate, and loving, we need to feel safe. If we are attracted to someone else, it is natural, but we can let it go; we don't have to act on those feelings. If we find ourselves wanting to act on our attractions, then we need to find out why. What are the underlying causes that are driving us to want to act this way? At this point it may be a good idea to consult a therapist to work the issue out privately, either with our partner or alone. We may need to dig deep to discover the reason behind our actions. Finding it may lead us in a more positive direction in our relationship rather than creating pain.

Infidelity doesn't work because:

- It runs counter to our cultural values.

- It's a betrayal of relationship trust.

- It deeply divides couples.

- It destroys our promise to be faithful.

- It can cause an enormous amount of pain.

- It is usually about something important that is going on within us or between us and our mate. Whatever it is, an affair won't fix it.

Monogamy works because:

- It creates and maintains trust.

- It upholds our relationship agreement.

- It creates peace and harmony.

- It adheres to a socially acceptable moral code.

- It supports relationship stability, safety, and security.

- It maintains intimacy.

- It preserves the emotional bond of truth and openness.

- We feel better about ourselves.

- It preserves honesty between us and our mate.

- No secrets means more intimacy.

Monogamy may not be easy, but that doesn't mean it's impossible. The challenge of being in a monogamous relationship is to become that kind of committed individual even when faced with desirable people around us. Relationships raise the bar for behavior that upholds our own values and protects the safety and security of our relationship. To be fully loving, caring, understanding, and kind, we must evolve; we must tussle with ourselves and our urges, our fantasies and our faults. To maintain love and keep from undermining it with pain and distrust, we have to rise to the ultimate relationship challenge and protect the trust that has been bestowed upon us. To break that trust will seriously damage the relationship and may even end it.

For Your Inter-Reflection

The Dynamics of Desire

1. What do you like about your sex life with your partner? How does sex enrich your relationship? Write down your favorite things about sex—including what makes you feel the best—and share them with your partner.

2. What would make your sex life better? What can you do to help?

3. Are there aspects of your sexual life that make you uncomfortable? Can you tell your partner about your discomfort?

4. How important is monogamy for your happiness in your relationship? How important is it to your partner? Can you talk about it?

5. Do you find yourself dreaming or fantasizing about others? How can you include those fantasies in your sex life with your partner?

6. Make a no-judgment pact with your partner. Then make a list of your sexual fantasies and ask your partner to do the same. Share your lists.

and they lived . . .

But you and I, love, we are together
from our clothes down to our roots:
together in the autumn, in water, in hips, until
we can be alone together—only you, only me.

—Pablo Neruda

TOLSTOY SAID THAT all happy families are alike—and while we can't claim that any one couple is like any other, it's true that couples who stay happy together have some significant things in common. From all the aspects of relationship that we've examined, let's see if we can sum up some of their secrets.

Couples who stay happy together are active, engaged, committed, and able to accept each other's influence, especially in times of stress and conflict. This dynamic process includes tolerance, patience, fairness, a sense of humor, and a willingness to be flexible with emotionally charged issues. People who are easygoing tend to let small spats roll off their backs and quickly bounce back from irritations and differences. Those who expect that love will conquer all or believe that their relationship is bulletproof are in for a surprise.

Couples who stay happy together make their relationship a high priority. They create time and space for tending to each other's needs; they take the trouble to look at things from each other's point of view, and also to look deeply within themselves so they will know who they are. They have a vision for their relationship and the resources to make it a reality. Because they know what they want from each other and what direction they're going in, they can actively create their own sense of excitement and possibility all along the way.

COLLABORATING ON HAPPINESS

Couples who stay happy together agree on what kind of relationship they want, not just on a philosophical but on a practical level. It's especially important to agree about social roles and how much time to spend together or with friends and family. How do we want to be with friends? How much sense does it make to take time away from each other? Does one person want to spend more time with family and friends than the other? Is it okay to have opposite-sex friends? Is it okay with our mate if we are friends with former lovers or ex-spouses? Who is going to work and who will stay home, or are both expected to work?

When we consider cultural and gender differences, morals, and values, we run into innumerable grounds for possible disagreement. Working out those issues one by one will help prevent future conflicts from arising. Some couples feel the same about friends and family and others do not. For example, many men (especially young men) want bonding time with their friends, while women tend to be more relationship-bound and often want time to socialize as a couple. This can lead to tension when their mates want to spend time alone with friends. If men aren't ready for the constraints of a relationship, women may feel neglected or left out. On the other hand, if women put on too much *pressure* and too many limits, men may become resentful. (And, of course, it can work the other way around as well.) Couples who beat the odds are able to find a balance between what each one wants and, in the process, actively create harmony.

Teamwork That Works

There is no one relationship style that works better than any other; the essential thing is to agree on what kind of relationship we want. Let's take a look at how this can work in our society's most traditional kind of relationship, in which one person stays at home, often taking care of the family, while the other works. A traditional relationship is usually bound by marriage, and as each person is occupied with quite different activities during the day, they have distinctly dissimilar desires for contact at night. The person coming home from a long day out in the world may want a break, while the person who has been alone all day may want to talk the minute the partner walks through the door. The partner who is in the workplace is getting paid, which is a positive affirmation. The stay-at-home partner, who may be doing childcare (which tends to be selfless), housework, and running errands, does not get as much external self-esteem support as the working parent does, so he or she may want more expressions of appreciation from the partner and feel slighted when they aren't forthcoming.

The stay-at-home partner tends to think more about the relationship because he or she is surrounded by reminders: spending much of the day in the home they share, having contact with other people who know them as a couple or a family. The partner who is working, in a different setting surrounded by different people, tends to think less about the other. If children are in the picture, the two partners' experiences are even more varied. The one who's been with the kids all day is tired and wants a break from childcare, while the other one wants to come home and relax after a hard day too. (We saw an example of this earlier in the book when a wife greeted her husband by handing over the baby: "You take her, I'm exhausted.") Couples who beat the odds find ways to allow for those differences, such as giving the person arriving home some time to decompress from the day, and then taking time to connect in the ways that are important to each one.

In a less traditional relationship model, both partners may work outside the home and share more similar sets of experiences. It's potentially easier for them to divide chores at home because the situation is more equal. Conflicts still occur in relationships where both people work, but they look a little different: perhaps one partner has a more stressful job or works longer hours or gets paid more than the other; perhaps one partner does more around the house. When couples become active participants in their relationship, they take the time to acknowledge each one's valuable contributions—and, on a practical level, to sit down and divide the chores. They might start by finding out what each person likes to do and work out an acceptable routine for getting things done. When couples learn to express concern, interest, and appreciation, and acknowledge each other's efforts to work as a team, they have a much better chance of making love last.

The Best of Everything

Bill and Lucy were college sweethearts. They married shortly after graduation and soon gave birth to a baby girl. Bill became a stockbroker. As he began to make large commissions, he and Lucy bought an old house and hastily began remodeling it, but it turned out to be a money pit that swallowed their finances at an alarming rate. At the same time, the stock market took a downturn, and they soon found themselves in hot water. They fought bitterly over the money that was pouring into the seemingly endless renovation. Bill wanted to please Lucy by giving her what she wanted, and she wanted the best of everything. But when the bills came in, he would blow a gasket.

Lucy couldn't understand what was making Bill so angry. After all, she was simply trying to make a beautiful home for him. He, in turn, was completely at a loss as to why Lucy needed everything to be top-of-the-line. Clearly, they were far apart in their sense of what they wanted their home—and their marriage—to be. Taking a look at their past promised to bring them closer to common ground as we unearthed the reason for Lucy's spending spree and Bill's difficulty with setting boundaries for spending.

Lucy had grown up in the poorest family in an affluent suburb. Her father, ashamed that he couldn't earn more money, compared himself unfavorably to his more well-heeled neighbors and hid his perceived inadequacy with ostentatious efforts to create the appearance of wealth. He was also arrogant and critical of everyone around him. Ultimately, he concealed the truth about the family's finances until they finally went bankrupt. So the value Lucy learned was that money equaled personal worth. Her father wanted her to marry into money, and she was anxious to please him and avoid his critical judgment. She dreamed of achieving wealth and social position so she could make up for her father's shame of never having enough. Once Lucy married Bill, her poor self-esteem drove her to buy expensive items for her house, just like her father's show of affluence to gain approval. The house became the symbol of her self-worth. She was determined to show the world that she was upper-class and therefore acceptable.

Bill's family, though more affluent than Lucy's, also placed a great deal of importance on having money. They owned a small business but made it seem to the world that it was more than it was. Bill's controlling mother pressured her children to go to college and major in business. His father was not only emotionally absent but a poor businessman, so his mother looked to Bill to be the family's savior. When she was angry with him, she would disappear into the business and withdraw from him. Because Bill's self-esteem was tied to his mother, these emotional disconnects made him insecure and fearful of abandonment, so when he met Lucy, he tried to make her happy as a way to keep her connected to him emotionally. He felt that the only way he could stave off being rejected as not good enough was to give Lucy everything she wanted. His self-esteem came to depend on never saying no to her. At the same time, he resented her for doing what she wanted. He secretly felt that she was with him only for the material advantages he gave her.

As the remodeling spun more and more out of control, Bill's self-esteem issues blocked him from telling Lucy that they couldn't afford what she was spending on the house. He believed that if she knew of their limited financial circumstances and his inability to meet her needs, she would leave him. So he lied to her about his money troubles, even as they fell deeper into debt, while behind the scenes he tried to work out deals to delay payments. Eventually, though, creditors began calling the house, and then Lucy found a pile of unpaid bills. Bill's worst fears were realized when Lucy threatened to leave him. She accused him of being a poor provider, weak, and a liar for trying to hide his troubles from her. She was full of contempt for Bill and, at the same time, terrified that someone would find out about their financial troubles.

They entered therapy on the brink of divorce. Slowly, they began to see the roots of the problems they were facing. Lucy was overcompensating for her low self-esteem by trying to create the perfect upscale home. Bill was trying to hold onto Lucy by giving her what she wanted, but couldn't keep up with her need for approval. As their deeper motivations became clear, they felt more compassionate toward each other, and they realized that to make their marriage work, they needed to come to a shared understanding of what they were doing and where they were going together. They devised a plan to pull themselves from the brink of financial ruin, and in the course of their struggle to become more financially stable, they realized that their family mattered more than anything else. They realized that spending money was not an adequate substitute for a life and was not a solution to their sense of personal deprivation; instead, their headlong drive to show the world how valuable they were was only making them angry and depressed. So Lucy agreed to a budget and Bill began a payment plan to reduce their debts. They worked on their relationship to make it more satisfying, and as they did, their need to spend decreased. They worked to develop a life together, and their efforts made their emotional connection stronger than ever.

AS WITHIN, SO WITHOUT

In his classic book *A Different Existence,* the phenomenologist J. H. van den Berg tells the story of a young man waiting in a mountain cabin for his lover to arrive. The room is aglow with light from the fireplace and bright with the young man's anticipation of meeting his true love in their hilltop hideaway. Beside him sits a bottle of wine. The wine appears beautiful to him through the prism of his desire; it glistens in the firelight as the whole room takes on the cast of this desire. Then the phone rings and he learns that his lover is not coming and will never come. Suddenly the fire appears menacing and the once glowing room seems gloomy and foreboding. The wine that only moments before appeared to be so divine now looks repulsive to him. But clearly nothing in the room has changed; it's only his feelings that have changed.

The Lens of Our Experience

Throughout this book, we have seen that our inner life affects the way we perceive what lies outside us. Jean-Paul Sartre said that reality is perspectival: it is our *perspective* that changes with the ebb and flow of emotion and then influences our sense of reality. Anaïs Nin put it this way: "We don't see things as they are. We see things as we are."

If our inner experience is depressed, fearful, insecure, and hateful, these struggles will taint our perception and affect our actions and reactions to ourselves and others. This effect is especially powerful in our intimate relationships. Once we grasp that our moods shape our perceptions and our responses to each other, we can pay attention to the way we are responding to our partner and vice versa and come to a valuable new understanding of our own perspective.

When a present experience mirrors our past, it stimulates what psychoanalyst Christopher Bollas terms an "emotional memory." In his book *The Shadow of the Object,* Bollas describes moods as emotional memories that represent a present stimulus to one of our early experiences. Our ability to understand what our moods are telling us about our history, and ultimately about ourselves, is critical to working through them. Distinguishing what's triggering our moods provides precious insight into what we're afraid of so we can work through it with our partner. Bringing old fears out of the darkness of our unconscious helps us to see that they're simply old memories and not present reality. In the same way, we can probe aspects of ourselves that Bollas describes as not quite unknown, but "unthought knowns." What he means by this is that we *know* that something is bothering us or that we feel less than others, but we don't really *think* about it. He believes that bringing those "unthought knowns" into consciousness allows us to process them, take the measure of our own subjectivity more fully and clearly, and eventually change the way we believe ourselves to be.

On Being an Objective Observer

The ability to observe ourselves from an objective point of view is an important part of relationship success. This means that we are seeing things as they actually are instead of through our often distorted subjectivity. Building objectivity works best when both people reflect together and create a sense of who they are within themselves and with each other. Without this objectivity, we are doomed to a subjective distortion that can pump out negativity into the system of our relationship. Children have not developmentally acquired the ability to be objective, so they always believe that they're responsible for the pain they feel. As children, we needed to keep an emotional connection with our parents to feel safe. As adults, we want to build an objective sense of the world and ourselves, which requires another person to reflect back to us what he or she sees. We need to trust what this person sees as truth and then process it as a part of who we are.

To be subjective as a child is essential for emotional survival. To be subjective as an adult can create conflict. Here's an example (with no sexism intended; it could just as easily be the other way around). A man is waiting for his wife to get ready, but she is running late as usual. He gets impatient and angrily protests, "Can't you ever be on time?" She snaps back at him, "I'm going as fast as I can." He counters, "It always has to be on your timetable; it's never about what I need." He could have predicted her response, yet he can't let it go. He berates her, and the argument becomes an exchange of furious insults and defensive remarks. In this deadlock of dark emotion, they become distant and silent. He feels that he is entirely justified because, after all, she's the one who is once again late. She, too, feels justified in getting angry, because he's overreacting so much.

Had he understood why he was so angry with her lateness, his initial response could have been short-circuited. Perhaps as a child he waited for his mother to pick him up from school and she often came late or forgot altogether. He might have a serious set of sad and angry feelings about lateness. If he knew this about himself, it could help him to respond differently to his wife's lateness and even find better solutions to the practical problem it presents. If he objectively understands that his wife is not abandoning him as his mother did—she's just a late person—then he will be less inclined to be so angry when she's late. He can decide to talk to her about the issue at a more conducive time, and they can come to some agreement about possible solutions. He may be able to busy himself with some worthwhile activity while he waits, and she may be able to plan better so that when she's ready they can leave unhurried. Building an objective view will help them to know where the pain is coming from so that they can avoid the problems the pain creates.

The cornerstone of all our interactions with others is our ability to recognize what we're experiencing within and then to apply that knowledge and perspective to the interaction at hand. The principles that seem to hold true are: *If we are self-critical, we will be critical with others. If we are depressed, our relationship will be depressed. If we feel insecure, we will bring insecurity into our relationship.* There is no way around how internal pain affects our relations with others. For this reason, self-knowledge is relationship power. Self-knowledge accesses relationships, and relationships access self-knowledge. An emotional bond with another person strengthens our ability to heal our personal wounds, to restore our sense of connection, and to create a safe place to love and be loved.

PARTNERS IN PROBLEM-SOLVING

The truth that many of us would like to resist is that to a great extent we control how people feel about us. This does not mean we must be phony: on the contrary, we must express how we truly and deeply feel with empathy, compassion, and kindness. Most couple discord occurs because we are too afraid to express our truth, so we become defensive or critical instead. Frequently I observe couples lashing out at each other when at the bottom of it they just want to know that the other one cares. They will get angry, blame, and act self-righteous about all kinds of things rather than risk their feelings being exposed. It's difficult for couples like these to peel back the layers and see that deep in their hearts they are just crying out for love. But if we are willing to risk being truthful about our feelings and are thoughtful, caring, and considerate in the way we do so, we are much more likely to resolve problems.

Mending Our Fences

When couples become dysfunctional, it's almost always because they don't know enough about who they are and how their personal issues are affecting their responses to each other. And when issues cycle around, it's usually because neither person will admit to his or her part in the problem, but goes on feeling entitled to be critical, angry, and blaming. When the victim becomes the aggressor, no resolution is possible. It becomes an endless tit-for-tat. More often than not, when I'm in treatment with a dysfunctional couple, it's because they're so focused on what the other one did wrong that they are unable or unwilling to see and/or admit what they are doing to create their 50 percent of the problem. If each person could own up to his or her part and acknowledge the feelings of the partner, most conflicts would promptly disappear.

It's also not unusual to find that people have no idea what lies deeply within them because their shame is hidden even from themselves. In therapy, once the deeper process is understood, we can work to heal the wound, and this will positively affect a couple's relationship: "Oh, I'm sorry that I hurt your feelings; I was hurt because I felt rejected and alone. I love you, I miss you, and I need you." This kind of dialogue uses conflict and complaining to create a new kind of connection.

Many couples find it difficult to resolve basic conflicts. But they needn't be in therapy to use these tools of self-examination and be truthful about their respective parts in the problem. To take this enlightened approach to an everyday quarrel, ask yourself the following questions:

- What is my responsibility in the current conflict?

- What are my partner's feelings and thoughts about the problem?

- Have I acknowledged what my partner is trying to tell me?

- Am I (or is my partner) in a bad mood, tired, or irritated about something else?

- What feelings, needs, and wants are being expressed?

- What could both of us do to make it better?

- What could we do differently next time?

To resolve conflicts we need to join with our mate in the problem-solving process. *When we become true partners, we recognize the need to put the welfare of the relationship before our particular point of view.* When we apologize to each other for any pain we have caused, we start to heal the broken connections that every relationship experiences. What's important is not that we will break connections—this is inevitable—but that we know how to repair them.

If we believe that bonds will never break, we are in for a disappointment. Loving kindness moves us toward each other, just as needing to be right and blaming moves us away. We do not have to find compassion first—we can find it along the way—but the important point is to look for it. To do so, we must risk exposing our hurt and vulnerability—an important step on the road to loving more deeply.

Staying the Course

What makes some couples persevere in difficult circumstances and others simply quit when the going gets tough? Couples who make love last are committed to working until a solution is reached. This may be done by striving to find a solution when the conflict occurs, or it may involve carefully orchestrated discussions over a period of time. It's important to persevere all the way to the end of a problem without losing our temper and becoming critical or contemptuous.

Working the problem all the way through is a way to internalize the solution so we don't encounter the same problem again. While it's true that personal issues don't go away altogether, our ability to understand and discuss those issues is critical to easing the tension arising from them. If we can see conflict as constructive and use it to set a direction or goal, we're on the right track.

It's important to realize that there are no quick fixes—at least none that work in the long run. Right now there's a flood of media-generated therapies offering fast and easy solutions to a whole host of psychological problems, ranging from marital conflicts to self-esteem issues. It's not that what these methods offer isn't helpful; the problem is that it's often only a piece of the truth, and those who take it for the whole truth may be disappointed. Finding lasting solutions often demands that we look deeper—not only in the therapist's office but in our everyday life with the one we love.

For Your Inter-Reflection

And They Lived . . .

1. Do you make your relationship a high priority in your life? Does your partner? Can you talk about the importance you give to your life together?

2. Think about the roles you and your partner play in your relationship. Is there a clear division of labor in your household? Are your roles traditional or nontraditional? Who decides what your roles are?

3. Describe how you work as a team. What do you do well? What would make your teamwork better?

4. On a scale of 1 to 10, how would you rate your "style" of interaction, intimacy, and conflict resolution? Does your partner rate them differently? Can you talk about how to improve them?

5. How are you going to stay happy together? Write down your thoughts and ask your partner to do the same, then share what you've written.

conclusion

Love must be as much a light as a flame.

—Henry David Thoreau

THE PRESSURE THAT COUPLES FACE in our modern culture is like none other in history. The fallout from everyday stresses and violent confrontations around the globe permeates our lives, and we witness this continually on the streets and in the news. Rising prices, shifts in the stock market, the competition for jobs, urban alienation, and the threat of terrorism are just some of the reasons for collective angst. If we find ourselves unable to develop and maintain a loving relationship amid these prevailing conditions, it adds even more strain to our all-too-taxing lives.

As couples face more obstacles than ever before, the pressure can seriously impact our connections with our loved ones, especially when we react with anger and rage to the difficulties we face. Angry couples become entangled in a negative cycle that may weaken—and perhaps eventually kill—even the most intense loving relationship. Caught up in the struggle for survival and success, we are vulnerable to the stress of competing in the workplace or the shame of feeling unable to do so. By the time we learn that the very struggle for fame or fortune frequently *adds* stress and undermines happiness, it may be too late.

So how can we heal the wounds of shame and rage, of early experience and present disappointment? Is there a cure for what ails our love? The answer is yes: what ails our love is what blocks it, and that is anger, criticism, withdrawal, and violence. So it would seem that whatever caused our wounds, the opposite might heal them. To find compassion instead of anger, understanding instead of criticism, affection and respect instead of neglect and distance, or loving empathy instead of loneliness, can build a connection that will last a lifetime.

As we saw in chapter 1, the pain in our relationships may run deep, but we have the C.U.R.E. at our fingertips.

Jean-Paul Sartre said that the past is determined by the future. I take this to mean that the more we're able to build a worthwhile life, the less concerned we will be with our painful past. Our childhood is a permanent record, a system unto itself. But we don't have to be imprisoned by it. Once we understand how our deepest wounds have affected the way we see ourselves and others, we are free to make choices about the way we want to live our lives. *We cannot change experience, but we can change our relationship to it.*

About ten years ago, when my father lay dying, we were alone at his bedside. He looked at me with great sincerity, and for the first time he told me that he was proud of me and that he loved me. He wanted to make it right between us. He wanted to make sure I knew. In that moment, all the pain that was between us—and there had been great pain—fell away, and I was left with only affection and compassion for him, tinged with amazement that love had reasserted itself so strongly here at the end.

The power of love comes back to me in the work I do, through all my own explorations, and within my marriage and my family. When it's all said and done, it appears that our ability to express and accept love is what makes life worth living. It is love, after all, that spins the ordinary into the extraordinary.

Love is the luminosity that lifts us from the drudgery of our everyday lives. To keep the flame of passion burning, couples need to reach beyond what feels safe, to risk rejection, in order to love more deeply. The work is to remove what blocks our ability to love and to encourage us to speak our truth and risk opening our hearts. A wise colleague of mine once said that there is no way to have a completely safe life and still live it.

The work of love is to create love. The goal is to make conflict resolution into intimacy creation. When we can depend on each other for understanding, caring, patience, perseverance, and tenderness, we make our relationship safe and secure. An apt metaphor to help us think about relationships is to liken them to the earth, with love being the atmosphere. When it's autumn, we prepare for impending challenges by making time for each other so that when winter does come, we can make a warm fire and keep out the cold. When it's spring, we celebrate. In the heat of summer, we seek the cool of a shade tree. We know when our relationship feels loving and the atmosphere is sweet. The goal is to keep our thoughts and feelings positive so we're living where the relationship temperature feels just right. When the climate between us is temperate and there is a soft breeze blowing in off the ocean of positive feelings, our lives feel uplifted. Knowing what to do when the weather changes can help maintain a loving atmosphere.

A patient once said to me that relationships are relentless. They are that and more. Who we are is before us, around us, between us, and between the lines. The truth is that if we want to love deeply, we cannot hide either from ourselves or from the ones we love. Love offers the ultimate challenge: not just accepting our own obvious imperfections, but also loving our partner not in spite of flaws but *because* of them. To reach into our souls and find the meaning in our current crisis is what lasting love and shared happiness require. If the question is "Why keep trying?", then the answer is our very willingness to open ourselves, to see ourselves through each other's understanding eyes, and to be lifted up again and again by the exquisite radiance of love.

REFERENCES

Ackerman, Diane. *A Natural History of Love.* New York: Vintage Books, 1995.

Ainsworth, Mary D. Salter. *Infancy in Uganda: Infant Care and the Growth of Love.* Baltimore: Johns Hopkins Press, 1967.

Anand, Margot. *The Art of Sexual Ecstasy: The Path of Sacred Sexuality for Western Lovers.* New York: Jeremy P. Tarcher, 1989.

Bach, George R., and Ronald M. Deutsch. *Pairing: How to Achieve Genuine Intimacy.* New York: Avon Books, 1971.

Barnes, Hazel E. *Humanistic Existentialism: The Literature of Possibility.* Lincoln, NE: University of Nebraska Press, 1959.

Barry, M. J. "Depression, Shame, Loneliness and the Psychiatrist's Position." *American Journal of Psychotherapy* 16 (October 1962): 580–90.

Beauvoir, Simone de. *The Second Sex.* New York: Knopf, 1990.

Berg, J. H. van den. *A Different Existence: Principles of Phenomenological Psychopathology.* Pittsburgh: Duquesne University Press, 1972.

Bernières, Louis de. *Corelli's Mandolin.* New York: Vintage Books, 1995.

Bollas, Christopher. *The Shadow of the Object: Psychoanalysis of the Unthought Known.* New York: Columbia University Press, 1989.

Bowlby, John. *Attachment and Loss, Volume I: Attachment.* New York: Basic Books, 1969.

Buss, David M. *Evolutionary Psychology: The New Science of the Mind.* Boston: Allyn & Bacon, 1998.

Cloke, Kenneth. *The Crossroads of Conflict: A Journey into the Heart of Dispute Resolution.* Calgary: Janis Publications, 2006.

Craske, Michelle G., and David H. Barlow. *Mastery of Your Anxiety and Panic: Therapist Guide.* 4th ed. New York: Oxford University Press, 2006.

Evans, Patricia. *Verbal Abuse Survivors Speak Out: On Relationship and Recovery.* Avon, MA: Adams Media, 2003.

———. *The Verbally Abusive Relationship: How to Recognize It and How to Respond.* 2nd expanded ed. Avon, MA: Adams Media, 2003.

Gilligan, Carol. *In a Different Voice: Psychological Theory and Women's Development.* 6th ed. Cambridge, MA: Harvard University Press, 1993.

Goffman, Erving. *The Presentation of Self in Everyday Life.* New York: Doubleday Anchor, 1959.

Gottman, John M., and Nan Silver. *The Seven Principles for Making Marriage Work: A Practical Guide from the Country's Foremost Relationship Expert.* New York: Crown, 1999.

Grosskurth, Phyllis. *Melanie Klein: Her World and Her Work.* Northvale, NJ: Jason Aronson, 1995.

Hite, Shere. *The Hite Report: A Nationwide Study of Female Sexuality.* New York: Dell, 1987.

Husten, Ted, John Coughlin, Renate Houtz, Shanna Smith, and Laura George. "The Connubial Crucible: Newlywed Years as Predictors of Marital Delight, Distress and Divorce." *Journal of Personality and Social Psychology* 80 (2001): 237–252.

Johnson, Susan M. *The Practice of Emotionally Focused Couple Therapy: Creating Connection.* 2nd ed. New York: Brunner-Routledge, 2004.

Jong, Erica. *Fear of Flying.* New York: Holt, Rinehart & Winston, 1973.

Karen, Robert. *Becoming Attached: First Relationships and How They Shape Our Capacity to Love.* New York: Oxford University Press, 1998.

Kaufman, Gershen. "The Meaning of Shame: Toward a Self-Affirming Identity." *Journal of Counseling Psychology* 21, no. 6 (1974): 568–574.

Kaufman, Gershen. *Coming Out of Shame: Transforming Gay and Lesbian Lives.* New York: Doubleday, 1995.

Kegan, Robert. *In Over Our Heads: The Mental Demands of Modern Life.* Cambridge, MA: Harvard University Press, 1998.

Kiersey, David, and Marilyn Bates. *Please Understand Me: Character & Temperament Types.* 5th ed. Del Mar, CA: Prometheus Nemesis Book Company, 1984.

Klein, Melanie, and Joan Riviere. *Love, Hate and Reparation.* New York: W. W. Norton & Company, 1964.

Kohlberg, Lawrence. *The Philosophy of Moral Development: Moral Stages and the Idea of Justice.* New York: Harper & Row, 1981.

Kundera, Milan. *The Unbearable Lightness of Being.* New York: HarperCollins, 2004.

Lévi-Strauss, Claude. *Tristes Tropiques.* New York: Criterion Books, 1961.

Malone, Thomas Patrick, and Patrick Thomas Malone. *The Art of Intimacy.* New York: Fireside, 1988.

Masters, William H., Virginia E. Johnson, and Robert C. Kolodny. *Masters and Johnson on Sex and Human Loving.* New York: Little, Brown & Company, 1988.

Mead, Margaret. *Sex and Temperament in Three Primitive Societies.* New York: Morrow, 1935.

Miller, Alice. *The Drama of the Gifted Child: The Search for the True Self.* 3rd ed. New York: Basic Books, 1996.

Mitchell, Stephen, ed. *The Enlightened Heart: An Anthology of Sacred Poetry.* New York: HarperPerennial, 1993.

Ofman, William V. *Affirmation & Reality: Fundamentals of Humanistic Existential Therapy and Counseling.* Los Angeles: Western Psychological Services, 1976.

Perel, Esther. *Mating in Captivity: Unlocking Erotic Intelligence.* New

York: Harper Paperbacks, 2007.

Siegel, Allen M. *Heinz Kohut and the Psychology of the Self.* New York: Routledge, 1996.

Solomon, Marion Fried. *Lean on Me: The Power of Positive Dependency in Intimate Relationships.* New York: Simon & Schuster, 1994.

Sullivan, Harry Stack. "Erogenous Maturation." *The Psychoanalytic Review* 12 (1926): 30.

Udry, J. Richard. *The Social Context of Marriage.* Philadelphia: J. B. Lippincott, 1966.

Wile, Daniel B. *Couples Therapy: A Nontraditional Approach.* New York: John Wiley & Sons, 1981.

Wurmser, Léon. *The Mask of Shame.* Northvale, NJ: Jason Aronson, 1997.

Yudofsky, Stuart C. *Fatal Flaws: Navigating Destructive Relationships with People with Disorders of Personality and Character.* Arlington, VA: American Psychiatric Publishing, 2005.

Dr. Bill Cloke has been a couples' therapist for 30 years. His passion is to help both individuals and couples lead more fulfilling lives and relationships by learning essential relationship skills. He received a master's degree in education from the University of Southern California and holds a PhD in psychology from California Graduate Institute. A frequent talk-radio psychologist, he is also a contributor to PsychologyToday.com and other popular websites and has lectured at UCLA. Bill Cloke lives with his wife in Los Angeles, where he works with couples, families, and children from a cross-section of cultures. To learn more about Bill Cloke, and for more resources on creating healthy, happy relationships, visit happytogetherbook.com.